The Concept of Integral Yoga according to Sri Aurobindo

The Concept of Integral Yoga according to Sri Aurobindo

S. Rajendran

SHARADA

Sharada Publishing House

DELHI

First Published 2011

ISBN: 978-81-88934-78-2
₹ 400

Published by:
SHARADA PUBLISHING HOUSE
111, Vidya Vihar Apartment
Sector - 9, Rohini, Delhi - 110 085
Ph.: +91-11-3292 1560, 2755 2102
E-mail: bansal_sph@rediffmail.com
Website: www.sharadabooks.com

Printed at:
Salasar Imaging Systems
Delhi

To My Revered Parents

Who made me what I am

Foreword

The whole world is a creation from Brahman. In the world thus created Brahman is seated as the Inhabitant. So there are two aspects of Brahman, the transcendent and the immanent. To realize Brahman in the two aspects is the goal of human life. The Isha (verse 14) points out that by the dual realization (*ubhayam saha*) one crosses death (*mrtyu*) and attains immortality (*amrtam asnute*). In fact, this is the significance of all creation – texts in the Upanishads.

Sri Aurobindo is a Vedantin who says that Brahman has descended into the world and become its inhabitant for the sake of manifesting Himself in the world and unfolding all latent powers through evolution. The evolution started with Matter. Then it reached Life and Mind. And man is a product of the evolution of Mind from Matter. Now two options are open to him: (i) to realize the twofold Brahman and be satisfied with it; (ii) to go ahead from this point and manifest the immanent Brahman, in himself and the world, through further evolution.

The Vedanta of the Upanishads is satisfied with the

first and does not pay attention to the second. Though this realization is good in itself, this is not the highest good for which man is eligible. Sri Aurobindo is the first Vedantin to invite us to go beyond the first option and arrive at the highest good by using the second option. To pass from Brahman to Brahman's purpose in the world is but a logical extension. Hence Sri Aurobindo's insistence upon reaching the highest good. He dedicated his whole life to this unique task. When we know that the immanent Brahman in Matter is the giver of the highest good, we do not speak ill of Matter but become a master who possesses and enjoys all hidden in Matter (*annavan annado bhavati*) (*Taittiriya Upanishad*, 3-7-1). If we are satisfied with the first option, then the goal can be realized through the yogas of works, knowledge and devotion. An isolated or a successive application of yoga is sufficient. If we desire to use the second option, the application of yoga must be "integral", otherwise the highest good cannot be realized. Sri Aurobindo's integral yoga is the result of this attempt.

Dr. Rajendran's work on the integral yoga of Sri Aurobindo is a good attempt. There are two merits to this work. First of all, it has established how Sri Aurobindo's integral yoga is derived from the metaphysics of integral Brahman. Secondly, it has proved how the components of integral yoga such as works (*karma*), knowledge (*jnana*) and devotion (*bhakti*) form a real synthesis by shedding their inherent limitations. Rajendran's expositions follow as closely as possible the original work, namely, *"The Synthesis of Yoga"* by Sri Aurobindo. Sri Aurobindo's yoga is new and a bold departure from the old yogas. These two features are well brought out by this work.

N. Jayashanmugam
Former Professor of Philosophy,
Sri Aurobindo International Centre of Education

Contents

Part - III
Philosophical Background of Integral Yoga

Part - IV
Nature of Integral Yoga

Part - V
Integral Yoga and the Concepts of Other Yogas

PREFACE

The aim of the present work is to expound Sri Aurobindo's conception of Integral Yoga with special reference to his fundamental work on this subject, 'The Synthesis of Yoga'.

Though in the last three decades numerous books on Sri Aurobindo have been published by several exponents of his thoughts, not many on Sri Aurobindo's Integral Yoga have appeared so far. In 1953, a work entitled 'The Integral Yoga of Sri Aurobindo' by Rishabhchand was published by Sri Aurobindo Ashram, Pondicherry. This was followed by another book with the title, 'Founding the Life Divine' (An introduction to the Integral Yoga of Sri Aurobindo) by Morwenna Donnelly. This was published in 1956 by a New York based publishing company. In 1961 a book on 'Sri Aurobindo's Integral Yoga' by Tulsidas Chatterjee was published by a Calcutta based publisher. In 1965 Prof. Haridas Chaudhuri brought out a book on 'Integral Yoga' which was a publication of George Allen and Unwin Ltd. These four works, which serve at the moment as the well known expositions on Sri Aurobindo's Yoga.

A study of Sri Aurobindo's treatise on Yoga 'The Synthesis of Yoga', will abundantly make it clear how the system of Integral Yoga has been conceived and expounded by its author. The book has been divided into four major sections with an introduction which deals with the conditions necessary for a synthesis of the existing systems of Yoga in India. Part I of the book deals with the Yoga of Works; part II with the Yoga of Knowledge; and Part III with the Yoga of Devotion. They respectively carry the following titles, 'The Yoga of Divine Works', 'The Yoga of Integral Knowledge' and 'The Yoga of Divine Love'. Part IV is a comprehensive exposition of the integral Yoga. It is called 'The Yoga of Self-Perfection'. Here, Sri Aurobindo clearly defines the nature and aim of the Integral Yoga and discusses the various stages that intervene between the beginning and the end. A cursory glance of the plan of the book and the main arguments of its chapters will be enough to understand that in all the four divisions the fourth and the last occupies a position of central importance. It is in this division that the distinctive features of the Integral Yoga have been outlined and elaborately described. In fact, it is the basis of the three foregoing divisions of the book. When Sri Aurobindo comments on the Yoga of Works or tells us that the Yoga is not be limited by the aim or the process of the traditional teachers, he does so in the light of what he has said in the fourth division of 'The Synthesis of Yoga'. This is true of other systems of Yogas as well. The essentials of the Integral Yoga, though separately formulated in the fourth division of Sri Aurobindo's book, appear in other divisions also when Sri Aurobindo tries to explain how a traditional system of Yoga gives up its narrow ideas and enters into the larger realm of integral Yoga. Therefore, if the reader is not alert and fails to keep in view the underlying purpose behind the plan of the first three divisions of the book, he is likely to believe that the theory of Integral Yoga is not an exclusive subject matter of any particular division, but a theme repeatedly stated in each division. This has led some exponents of Sri Aurobindo's Yoga to think that the integral Yoga can be understood even if some of the divisions of Sri Aurobindo's book are not taken into account. In fact, it is a serious misconception which the present work tries to avoid.

Apart from the basic treatise, 'The Synthesis of Yoga', Sri Aurobindo has written many other works which also have a bearing on his Yoga. In these works, he has either explained some of the important ideas on Integral Yoga or indicated how some of the components of his Yoga are derived from certain traditional systems. For example, there are a few works on Yoga by Sri Aurobindo such as 'Bases of Yoga', 'The Yoga and its Objects', 'Lights on Yoga' and 'More Lights on Yoga'. In these works, Sri Aurobindo explains some of the aspects of Yoga from the practical point of view without trying to comprehensively expound the nature of the Integral Yoga. Similarly, 'Essays on the Gita' is mainly a commentary and secondarily an attempt to indicate that some of the components of integral Yoga are traceable to the *Gita*. A third category includes Sri Aurobindo's 'Letters on Yoga' which are a collection of letters written to *sadhakas* on various questions relating to the practice of his Yoga. Some authors who have written works on Sir Aurobindo's Integral Yoga lost sight of the basic distinction between primary and secondary works and concentrated on the latter works rather than on the former ones. This is also another grave misconception which the present work is trying to eliminate.

Morwenna Donnelly's book 'Founding the Life Divine' is unique in the sense that it is a book written with a view to convince that even non-oriental can practice oriental Yoga. Though the book claims to be an introduction to the integral Yoga of Sri Aurobindo, the author has completely neglected Sri Aurobindo's basic work, 'The Synthesis of Yoga', and relied mainly on the secondary works such as 'Letters', 'The Yoga and its objects', 'Bases of Yoga', 'More Lights on Yoga' and 'Essays on the Gita'. It is true that, there are one or two references to 'The Synthesis of Yoga' but she uses them only to focus our attention on the need to get rid of egoism. Though elimination of egoism is an important element in the Integral Yoga, there are equally or more important elements in 'The Synthesis of Yoga' which are essential and cannot be left out. The book in question is an example of how a work on the Integral Yoga has been written without drawing upon the ideas embedded in a basic work on the subject.

'Sri Aurobindo's Integral Yoga' by Tulsidas Chatterjee, like the book mentioned above, is largely based on the secondary works of Sri Aurobindo. In fact, some of its chapters are based on materials found in 'The Life Divine' which is a work on metaphysics. However, this book unlike the previous one, draws upon 'The Synthesis of Yoga' to a considerable extent. For example, the chapters 'Purification of the Nature' (p. 145), 'The Yoga of Self-Perfection' (p. 270), 'The Yoga of Divine Work' (p. 162), 'The Yoga of Divine Knowledge' (p. 177) and 'The Yoga of Divine Love' (p. 187) are based upon the primary work 'The Synthesis of Yoga'. Unfortunately, in none of these chapters the author has projected the basic point of view from which Sri Aurobindo wrote the corresponding chapters of his book. For example, in his chapter on 'The

Yoga of Divine Work' (p. 162) he has failed to point out how the Yoga of works, when stripped of its limitations, merges into the integral Yoga. This comment is equally valid in respect of his other chapters also. His chapter on 'The Yoga of Self-Perfection' (p. 270), though meant to be a brief statement of the corresponding chapter in Sri Aurobindo's work, stands apart and does not indicate how it is an indispensable section on the subject of the book.

'Integral Yoga' by Haridas Chaudhuri is a very elementary book and does not touch upon real components of Sri Aurobindo's Yoga. The three chapters which form the central idea of the book are the chapters three to five. In third and forth chapters, 'The Synthesis of Yogas' (p. 53), the author shows how the traditional Yogas are limited and exclude each other without entering into any harmonious pattern. He goes on to point out that Sri Aurobindo's Yoga removes their limitations and creates a harmonious system which includes the valuable elements of other Yogas. In this respect, these chapters are closer to the spirit of Sri Aurobindo's work. But chapter fifth, 'Basic Principles of Integral Yoga' (p. 83) has very little to say on what Sri Aurobindo has actually described in the 'Yoga of Self-Perfection'.

'The Integral Yoga of Sri Aurobindo' by Rishabhchand is also similar in some respects to the books referred previously. This book also largely relies on the secondary sources such as 'Letters on Yoga', 'Essays on the Gita', 'The Life Divine' and other works like 'Bases of Yoga'. However, this book, unlike the other books, recognizes the importance of 'The Synthesis of Yoga' and a considerable portion of it is directly based on the materials of primary work. The author brings out very clearly how Yogas of *karma, jnana* and *bhakti* shed their limitations and become harmonious in Sri Aurobindo's

Yoga. Though, in Sri Aurobindo's main work, the aspect of *siddhi* or perfection is considered to be as important as *suddhi* and *mukti* (purification and liberation), Rishabhchand does not pay attention to it except as an element of the Yoga of works (p. 229). In this respect, the book in question does not seem to have attached a major importance to Sri Aurobindo's main work on the Integral Yoga.

The present work, "The Concept of Integral Yoga: According to Sri Aurobindo", is written with a view to overcome the deficiencies of the books mentioned above. It proceeds on the assumption that the Integral Yoga could be expounded on the basis of Sri Aurobindo's main work without depending on his secondary works.

There are five parts to the present work. Part I presents a Biographical account of Sri Aurobindo. Part II introduces the subject by pointing out the possibility of combining the traditional systems of yoga and arriving at a larger result. It consists of three chapters. Chapter 1 gives an account of the various traditional systems of yoga. It stresses the need for their synthesis. Chapter 2 deals with the *Gita* as interpreted by Sri Aurobindo and shows how the triple yoga (works, knowledge and devotion) is given a synthetic outlook by the *Gita*. Chapter 3 gives a broad outline of the basis and principles of harmonizing the traditional systems of Yoga.

Part III explains the metaphysical background of Integral Yoga. This is based on Sri Aurobindo's metaphysical *magnum opus*, 'The Life Divine'. Since, the metaphysical part of Sri Aurobindo's Yoga is taken for granted in the chapters on 'The Synthesis of Yoga,' it becomes necessary to state the metaphysical part clearly. It seeks to avoid the extremes of materialism and asceticism. It focuses on the reality of Brahman out of which the world is born and for which the world exists and evolves. It explains that man is a concealed God and his ultimate aim is to discover and express it under the conditions of the earthly life. Sri Aurobindo foresees the emergence of a new humanity possessing spiritual light as a natural endowment in the society. Its aim is to convince in rational terms the possibility of spiritual perfection of humanity.

Part IV is an exposition of Sri Aurobindo's conception of Integral Yoga as outlined in the section entitled 'The Yoga of Self-Perfection'. Sri Aurobindo says that, human personality consists of several parts and all these parts have to be integrated into a harmonious unity. He speaks of four levels of accomplishing this grand integration :

1. Purification of the mental and vital parts.

2. Liberation of the soul from its subjection to the play of the three *gunas*.

3. Perfection and establishment of equality in all parts of our personality.

4. Free participation in the Divine work and Divine enjoyment. This part concentrates on the first three stages alone, as the section on 'The Yoga of Self-Perfection' is left incomplete by Sri Aurobindo.

Thus, the five chapters concentrate on the integral yoga proper.

Part V is an attempt to reinterpret the basic ideas of other yogas and extend their connotations in the light of Sri Aurobindo's Yoga. It consists of four chapters. Chapter 10 points out that self-giving, elimination of ego and service to the Divine are the three important elements of the yoga of works which acquire new connotations.

Chapter 11 says that the infinite Brahman is the goal of yoga of knowledge. Concentration, renunciation, absence of ego, oneness, liberation and samadhi are the most important elements that acquire extended significances. Chapter 12 focuses on the Yoga of devotion. It represents the culmination of the Yoga of works and the yoga of knowledge. Chapter 13 is a brief statement on Hathayoga, Rajayoga and Tantrayoga, in which the ideas of physical perfection, absorption in the self and cosmic enjoyment come to possess fresh significances. Thus, in part V, important concepts of traditional yogas are interpreted in the light of Sri Aurobindo's Yoga.

Acknowledgements

I take this opportunity to offer my deep sense of gratitude to Dr. S.P. Adhinarayan, former Vice-Chancellor, Prof. and Head, Department of Philosophy, Annamalai University, who was kind enough to admit me as a Research Scholar under his guidance. I sincerely thank my revered teacher and guide Dr. R. Kolappa Pillai, Reader in Philosophy, Annamalai University. My contact with this teacher of great compassion and deep spirituality proved a boon to my life. His affectionate guidance and encouragement have enabled me to complete my work.

I express my sincere gratitude and indebtedness to my teacher Dr. N. Jayashanmugam, a renowned authority on Sri Aurobindo's Philosophy who helped throughout my research work. It is difficult for me to acknowledge in words the immense benefit I have derived from his invaluable help and guidance.

I am also in deep obligation and gratitude to my Professors, Mr. C. Ramalingam, Dr. V. Rathinasabapathi and the faculty members who are presently working in the Department of Philosophy for their constant encouragement and facilities provided for my research work.

I am grateful to my esteemed friend Dr. A. Appan Ramanujam, former Head of the Department of Philosophy, Vivekananda College, Chennai for his keen interest in bringing out this volume.

I am deeply obliged to Dr. J. Rangaswami, Director, School of Philosophy, Tamil University, Thanjavur and Dr. S. Kotandaraman, Professor of Shastras, Raja's College, Tiruvaiyaru for their help in bringing out this work.

I am thankful to my wife Mrs. R. Savithiri, my son Dr. R. Aravindan and my daughter Dr. (Mrs.) Ramya Vimalathithan for their constant encouragement to complete this work.

I offer my grateful thanks to the most respectable Pro-Chancellor Dr. M.A.M. Ramasamy, Dr. M. Ramanathan, Vice-Chancellor and Dr. M. Rathinasabapathi, Registrar, Annamalai University and other University authorities for permitting me to publish this work.

Finally, I am also grateful to Sharada Publishing House, Delhi for publishing this work with great care and neatness.

ABBREVIATIONS

S.Y.	-	The Synthesis of Yoga
L.D.	-	The Life Divine
B.G.	-	The Bhagavad Gita
E.G.	-	Essays on the Gita

Part - I
A Biographical Sketch of Sri Aurobindo

Sri Aurobindo — A Biographical Sketch

Sri Aurobindo's father Dr. Krishna Dhan Ghose was born in 1845. He married Swarnalatha Devi, the eldest daughter of Rishi Rajnarain Bose. Rajnarain Bose was referred to the "grand-father of Indian Nationalism". In 1869, Dr. Krishna Dhan Ghose left for Great Britain for advanced medical studies. In 1871, he returned to India and became one of the most successful civil surgeons of his days.

Sri Aurobindo was born on 15th August, 1872 as the third son of his parents. His father decided to give his children European type of education. Because he believed, like many Indians in those days, that the English character was ideal. So, all his children were sent to Loretto Convent School at Darjeeling in 1877. Sri Aurobindo was 5 years old at that time. In 1879, the children were taken to England and entrusted to an English family, Mr. and Mrs. Drewett. Dr. Krishna Dhan left strict instructions with the Drewett that the children should be kept away from any

Indian influence. In 1884, Sri Aurobindo was admitted to St. Paul's School and was there till 1889. Sri Aurobindo was making an impressive progress in all his subjects of study including Greek and Latin. During the last two years at St. Paul's school Sri Aurobindo was registered as a candidate for the Indian Civil Service examination. In 1882, he passed the first part of the I.C.S. examination but for reasons known only to Sri Aurobindo did not pay attention to the riding test which was an essential aspect of the I.C.S. examination. In 1892, Sri Aurobindo had an interview with the Gaikward of Baroda who was then on a visit to England. The Gaikward appointed him as an officer in the Baroda state service.

Sri Aurobindo left England by a boat called Carthage for India. At that time another boat went down off the coast of Portugal and many passengers were lost. It was wrongly reported to Dr. Krishna Dhan that Sri Aurobindo's boat was lost and he was one of the victims. The news came as a stunning blow to Dr. Krishna Dhan and he died the same day. After a gap of 14 years Sri Aurobindo set foot on the soil of India. When he landed in Bombay, a vast calm descended upon him and remained for long months afterwards.

Sri Aurobindo spent about 13 years in the Baroda state service, from 1893 to 1907. During this period, he was in so many positions. In 1904, he became Principal of the Baroda College.

Apart from his service at the Baroda state, he was also deeply interested in the political situation of the country. He was contributing articles to the *Indu Prakash* of Bombay under the title "New Lamps for Old". The Editor introduced the series to the readers in the following words.

Hypocrisy has been the besetting sin of our political agitation. Oblique vision is the fashion. True, matter of fact, honest criticism is very badly needed… The questions at issue are momentous. It is the making or the unmaking of the nation. We have, therefore, secured a gentleman of great literary talents, of liberal culture and of considerable experience, well versed in the art of writing, at great personal inconvenience and probable misrepresentation, to give out his views in no uncertain voice and... in a style and direction peculiarly his own. We... assure them (our readers) that they will find in these articles matter that will set them thinking and stir their patriotic souls.[1]

In 1910, Sri Aurobindo came to Bengal and met the revolutionaries who worked for India's freedom. He favoured an open armed revolution in the whole of India in order to put an end to the British rule. He became an important leader of the revolutionary groups that were operating in India, though he did not openly plunge into the political movement as he was still in state service of Baroda.

Perhaps parallel to Sri Aurobindo's involvement in politics his involvement in spiritual practices was gradually developing. He was impressed by Swami Brahmananda of Ganga Math on the banks of the Narmada and a Naga Sannyasi who cured the malignant fever from which his brother Barin was suffering and which proved unresponsive to medical treatment. Sri Aurobindo was practicing *pranayama* for about five hours a day. The results were amazing and Sri Aurobindo was convinced of the tremendous powers that lie unused in the human being. He thought that he could utilize these powers for successful political action.

About 1906, Sri Aurobindo decided to give up his service at Baroda state and directly plunge into politics.

He was contributing revolutionary articles to "*Bande mataram*", but subsequently, he took over the editorship of the daily. The daily became very popular and produced immense impact on the Indian people. He was setting forth a political philosophy and action which drew its strength from our religious traditions. He described the work of national emancipation as a great and a holy *yajna*. He said that, the motherland was a goddess who loved not an imperfect sacrifice, a grudging giver. He called upon the people to offer all that they had into the fire of the *yajna*, feeding the fire ever with their blood and lives and happiness of their nearest and the dearest. He declared that the country should base itself on a political vedantism. He said:

> Our attitude is a political Vedantism. India, free, one and indivisible, is the divine realization to which we move, emancipation our aim... Passive resistance may be the final method of salvation in our case or it may be only the preparation for the final *sadhana*. In either case, the sooner we put it into full and perfect practice, the nearer we shall be to national liberty.[2]

Such inspired writings of Sri Aurobindo awakened the Indian population to the urgent need for a radical political action in the country. This created problems not only with the Moderates of the Nationalist Movement but also with the British bureaucracy. While Moderates considered him as a major obstacle on the path of freedom, and the British government looked upon him as a very dangerous person, because his hold on the people was hypnotic, his writings and actions had always a deliberate form which eluded the attempts of the British government to accuse Sri Aurobindo of anti-British activities. But the British government was trying its best to find an excuse to arrest Sri Aurobindo and put him permanently in prison for a criminal act from which he could not escape. When the revolutionaries threw a bomb at a closed carriage that was supposed to carry kingsford, a district Magistrate, the bomb actually killed two innocent ladies, Mrs. and Miss. Pringle Kennedy. Using this occasion, the British government arrested Sri Aurobindo and accused him of conspiracy in Muzzaferpore tragedy which later came to be called the "Alipur bomb case". This took place in the year 1908.

Sri Aurobindo, though he knew the evil designs of the British government did not think that he would be implicated in a conspiracy case like this. By this time, Sri Aurobindo had developed immense faith in the power of God to protect him for the great work he undertook. Therefore, he cried to Him for help. He says:

> When I was arrested and hurried to the Lal Bazar *hajat*, I was shaken in faith for a while, for I could not look into the heart of His intention. Therefore, I faltered for a moment and cried out in my heart to Him, "What is this that has happened to me? I believed that I had a mission to work for the people of my country and until that work was done, I should have Thy protection. Why then am I here and on such a charge?" A day passed and a second day and a third, when a voice came to me from within, 'Wait and see'. Then, I grew calm and waited. I was taken from Lal Bazar to Alipur, and was placed for one month in a solitary cell apart from men. There I waited day and night for the voice of God within me, to know what He had to say to me, to learn what I had to do. In this seclusion, the earliest realization, the first lesson came to me.[3]

Sri Aurobindo took the occasion to leave the entire case in the hands of the Divine and concentrate on the *sadhana* of the *Gita*. One day, the vision that all was Brahman, all was Vasudeva unfolded itself to him, and he saw Vasudeva everywhere. When he was taken to the court and produced before the Magistrate, he saw the same Vasudeva in the Magistrate and everybody else. Recalling this experience he says:

> I looked and it was not the Magistrate whom I saw, it was Vasudeva, it was Narayana who was sitting there on the bench. I looked at the prosecuting counsel... it was Sri Krishna who sat there, it was my Lover and Friend who sat there and smiled. "Now do you fear?" He said: "I am in all men and I overrule their actions and their words. My protection is still with you..."[4]

The case took its own natural course and Sri Aurobindo did nothing even to prepare his defense counsel. Suddenly, one day Chittaranjan Das decided to take up the defense of Sri Aurobindo and plead on his behalf. This Chittaranjan Das did on his own without anybody's request, either from Sri Aurobindo himself or from anyone who was closely associated with Sri Aurobindo. The defense counsel spent days and nights working on the case even to the extent of spoiling his health. He spoke very eloquently about the accused and pleaded that the accused was totally innocent and had nothing to do with the Muzzaferpore tragedy. The Magistrate after listening to the arguments from both sides waited for the verdict of the Assessors. The unanimous verdict was "Not Guilty". Accepting the verdict Mr. Beachcroft, the judge acquitted Sri Aurobindo. This was on 14th April, 1909.

After he was acquitted in the case, Sri Aurobindo started two weekly papers, the *Karmayogin* in English and *Dharma* in Bengali in order to rekindle the fervour and passion for national emancipation among his country men. He was going from place to place making speech after speech, with unparalleled vigour and enthusiasm. Some of his speeches were inspired and prophetic. And in his 'Uttarpare speech', he spoke of his experience of Divine omnipresence in the jail and outside, and his commitment to India's '*Sanatana Dharma*'. In January, 1910, a Deputy Superintendent of Intelligence Department was shot down on the steps of the High Court publicly and under the eyes of many by a boy of twenty. News came to Sri Aurobindo that he was likely to be arrested again, for the British government was really waiting for another opportunity to posit a case on Sri Aurobindo and some how put an end to his political career. While he was listening to the news, Sri Aurobindo received a clear divine command from within "Go to Chandernagore". A boat was immediately engaged and Sri Aurobindo boarded it, and it made for Chandernagore.

Chandernagore was Sri Aurobindo's transient "Inn of Tranquility" where his spiritual life took a new turn. He had experiences...

> A Voice Cried, "Go where none has gone!
> Dig deeper, deeper yet
> Till thou reach the grim foundation stone
> And knock at the keyless gate..."

That seemed to mark a definite advance in his *Yoga Sadhana*. He was confronted with a totally new situation, a spiritual difficulty the resolution of which held a promise of an unheard of change in earthly life. But, he could not stay in Chandernagore for a long time, because he received another divine command which asked him to go to Pondicherry. There he would have his "Gave of *Tapasya*", and there he would build his *sadhanalaya*. Sri Aurobindo left Chandernagore incognito and arrived in Pondicherry on 4th April, 1910. Since then, he stayed in Pondicherry until he passed away in 1950. The mysterious circumstance of Sri Aurobindo's disappearance raised several doubts in the minds of his own admirers and of the top level officers who were trying to arrest Sri Aurobindo. Sri Aruobindo was only waiting for a right moment to announce that he had come to Pondicherry, because he felt he was obliged to inform his country men who were interested in his where abouts. Apart from this, he wanted to tell his political enemies that he was no longer interested in political life for its own sake. He published a note about himself in one of the leading English dailies of Madras.

> I shall be obliged if you will allow me to inform every one interested in my whereabouts through your journal that I am and will remain in Pondicherry. I left British India over a month before proceedings were taken against me and, as I had purposely retired here in order to pursue my yogic *sadhana* undisturbed by political action or pursuit and had already severed connection with my political work, I did not feel called upon to surrender on the warrant for sedition, as might have been incumbent on me if I had remained in the political field. I have since lived here as a religious recluse, visited only by a few friends, French and Indian, but my whereabouts have been an open secret, long known to the agents of the government and widely rumoured in Madras as well as perfectly known to every one in Pondicherry. I find myself now compelled, somewhat against my will, to give my presence here a wider publicity.[5]

One of the events that marked the major turning

point in our cultural history is the appearance of a philosophical magazine called '*Arya*'. In the first issue of the monthly was released on 15th August 1914. The *Arya* placed before itself had a two-fold objects: (1) "a systematic study of the highest problems of existence", and (2) "the formation of the vast synthesis of knowledge, harmonizing the diverse religious traditions of humanity occidental as well as oriental".[6] The last issue of the '*Arya*' to appear was January, 1921. It carried Sri Aurobindo's writings on various subjects. All his major works such as 'The Life Divine', 'The Secret of the Veda', 'The Synthesis of Yoga', 'The Ideal of Human Unity', 'The Human Cycle', 'Essays on the Gita', 'Foundations of Indian Culture' and Future Poetry filled the pages of the *Arya* month after month. It was really a Herculean task to write on so many themes simultaneously, an achievement which had no parallel in the history of creative writing. The ideas and the teachings of Sri Aurobindo introduced an entirely new perspective in Indian culture.

Another event which figured as a landmark in the spiritual history of India is the founding of an *ashram* in the name of Sri Aurobindo. It came into existence to establish two important things: (1) yoga and life are not opposed to each other, and (2) the idea of a yoga which is not divorced from life must prepare for the appearance of the new humanity. The *ashram* is, therefore, a first step in giving a concrete shape to the teachings of Sri Aurobindo. The *ashram* was established sometimes after the arrival of the Mother in 1922.

A third event in Sri Aurobindo's life after his arrival in Pondicherry is the descent of a higher Divine consciousness in the physical body of Sri Aurobindo. This took place on 24th November, 1926. This was called the "Victory Day", because Sri Aurobindo thought that this would help in the long-run the descent of the original creative power of the Divine into the physical substance of the world. Sri Aurobindo went into seclusion in order to work on this possibility. Till 1950, he continued his efforts to bring down the Divine consciousness and power into the heart of inconscient Matter. It was no easy work, because he had to struggle against an enormous resistance which physical Matter had possessed as its original property. The more he delved deep into Matter the more assailed he was by its dark forces. The resistance finally precipitated into a crisis of physical death for Sri Aurobindo. He saw that unless he allowed the possibility of the physical death as a strategy he could not take the Divine light into the heart of Matter. The result was Sri Aurobindo gave up his physical body on 5th December, 1950. In proof of his success in bringing the Divine light into Matter, his body was emitting a golden light continuously for three days and did not show any sign of decomposition until 9th December, 1950.

REFERENCES

1. K.R. Srinivasa Iyengar, Sri Aurobindo (a biography and a history), Sri Aurobindo International Centre of Education, Pondicherry, vol. I, pp. 97-98.
2. *Ibid.*, pp. 389-390.
3. *Ibid.*, p. 553.
4. *Ibid.*, p. 558.
5. *Ibid.*, p. 663.
6. *Ibid.*, p. 708.

Part - II
Traditional Systems and their Synthesis

CHAPTER 1

TRADITIONAL SYSTEMS OF YOGA

Yoga as a Special Application of Nature's Method

Though Yoga appears to be something mystic or abnormal which has no relation to the ordinary process of life, it is really an intense and exceptional use of powers that life has already manifested. In this sense, any system of Yoga is but a selection of a particular element in general methods which Nature uses loosely and largely in order to achieve an upward movement. What Nature does in leisurely movement with an apparent waste of material energy, Yoga achieves the same goal with a greater intensity in shorter duration. It is appropriate to recall Swami Vivekananda's definition of Yoga as "a means of compressing one's evolution into a single life or a few years or even a few months of bodily existence".

The contact of the individual consciousness with the Divine is the essence of Yoga. The contact may take place at any point in our personality: in the physical through the body or in the vital through the nervous being or in the mental through the emotional heart or the active will or the understanding mind. The type of Yoga is determined by the point of contact in the human personality.

The Traditional Systems

Though there are many schools of Yoga some of them are considered to be very important both for their effectivity and utility. In Sri Aurobindo's view they are not exclusive or opposed to each other. They are really complimentary. Speaking about this aspect of different schools of Yoga Sri Aurobindo writes:

> "If, leaving aside the complexities of their particular processes, we fix our regard on the central principle of the chief schools of Yoga still prevalent in India, we find that they arrange themselves in an ascending order which starts from the lowest rung of the ladder, the body, and ascends to the direct contact between the individual soul and the transcendent and universal Self. Hathayoga selects the body and the vital functionings as its instruments of perfection and realization; its concern is with the gross body. Rajayoga selects the mental being in its different parts as its lever-power; it concentrates on the subtle body. The triple path of Works, of Love and of Knowledge uses some part of the mental being, will, heart or intellect as a starting point and seeks by its conversion to arrive at the liberating Truth, Beatitude and Infinity which are the nature of the spiritual life. Its method is a direct commerce between the human Purusha in the individual body

and the divine Purusha who dwells in every body and yet transcends all form and name."[1]

He finds that each system of Yoga is unique in so far as it achieves the result by concentrating on one particular aspect of our personality. There is a close parallel between the conception of personality and the type of Yoga one chooses to follow.

Hathayoga

Hathayoga is a system which starts with the body. According to this Yoga, body is not "a mere mass of living matter but a mystic bridge between the spiritual and the physical being."[2] The aim of hathayoga is to conquer life and body. During normal span of human life the usual amount of vital or dynamic force required to maintain the physical engine is sufficient. But for a *Yogic* purpose it is insufficient. Therefore, the physical and nervous part of our personality is subjected to a severe discipline which allows the inrush of a greater vital energy. This is accomplished in two stages:

(1) Normally, the body is restless. It is an indication of its inability to contain vital forces that come from the universal source. *Asana* liberates the body and the vital part from their habits which keep man within the narrow limit of normal operations.

(2) *Pranayama* is the next step. It makes two things possible:

(a) It helps to get robust health, prolonged youth and an extraordinary longevity.

(b) It awakens the coiled up serpent power and opens the individual to higher levels of consciousness and existence.

Rajayoga

Rajayoga aims at the control of emotional and sensational life. It is difficult to master thought and consciousness without the control of emotional life. Like hathayoga, rajayoga concentrates on the purification of its main instrument and tranquillizes it. The normal constitution of human mind is subjected to trouble and disorder. Nothing great can be achieved in the condition of trouble and disorder. Therefore the powers of order must come into existence and replace those of disorder. The powers of order come into existence when mind is subjected to a careful self-discipline. Practice of truth, renunciation of egoistic seeking, abstention from injury to others, constant meditation create a clear state of mind and heart. Once the disorder is removed, absolute quietness of mind and sense must be established. By using *asana* and *pranayama*, perfect quietness of the mind is achieved. Though, *asana* and *pranayama* are hathayogic devices, they are not used in their original forms, they are used only to the extent that to sub-serve the purpose of this system of Yoga. The ordinary restless mind is elevated to a higher level through practice of *samadhi*.

Tantrayoga

Tantra is an ancient system of yoga which seeks to combine some of the valuable elements of rajayoga and hathayoga. Like hathayoga, it awakens the coiled up force in the subtle body and takes it gradually to the highest centre of consciousness from *Muladhara* to *Sahasrara*. But in this process, it does not follow the intricate physical exercises of hathayoga. Like rajayoga, it also aims at a supreme state of *samadhi* where the *kundalini shakti* becomes one with *Paramasiva*. There is also another sense in which it is similar to rajayoga. It believes that outer nature is to be controlled and conquered. Though rajayoga and hathayoga ultimately envisage renunciation of world, the *tantra* does not. Since, the world itself is an expression of Siva, the existence of soul in the world after releasing the unification of *Shakti* with Siva, is not alienated from its Divine origin. Talking of the value of desires in the *tantra*. Sir John Woodroffe writes: "All these desires ultimately come from the divine will. In the final analysis they are aids to the process of evolution and progress. The important thing is to fulfill them with that understanding in a spirit of co-operation with the creative force of evolution. The creative force of evolution is no other than the divine will immanent in the world process. The more a person co-operates with the evolutionary impetus, the more his desires are purged of the egoistic taint and are transmuted into the pure flame of aspiration for divine life."[3]

The Triple Path

The triple path of devotion, knowledge and works concentrates on the three powers of consciousness rather than on the stuff of consciousness. Whereas rajayoga occupies itself with an elaborate system of discipline as the condition of perfection, the triple path concentrates on one of the central powers and converts it by turning away from its ordinary activity and fixing it on the Divine. The path of knowledge uses the method of *vicara* and *viveka,* intellectual reflection and right discrimination. The different elements of our phenomenal existence are distinguished and subsequently rejected as constituents of phenomenal nature, *prakriti* or *maya*. With the rejection of the phenomenal Nature, right identification with the true self which is not mutable or perishable becomes possible. In practice, the rejection of the phenomenal Nature takes an extreme form when the Nature is dismissed as an illusion. The goal of this Yoga is achieved when the individual soul dissolves itself in the supreme without return. The path of devotion has the enjoyment of Supreme Love and Bliss as the final goal. It looks upon the supreme Being as the divine Lover and Enjoyer of the Universe. The world is divine play of the Lord. There is not only self-concealment but self-revelation. In man, God reveals himself more fully than in other beings. Naturally, the play at human level takes a fundamental turn in the process of self-revelation. All normal relations of human life into which emotion enters are used in seeking the Divine Lover. All these relations apply no longer to transient worldly objects. They now apply to the joy of the All-Loving Divine Being. A unique feature of this Yoga is that even enmity and opposition to God becomes a means of realization and salvation. The goal of the path of works is to dedicate every human activity to Divine will. It gives up all egoistic aim for our works. Nothing is pursued for the sake of the worldly result. This purifies the mind and the will. The consciousness of the universal energy as the real doer of all our actions comes to surface. One becomes aware that the Lord of the Universal energy is the ruler with the individual as only an instrument or a mask. When one realizes the complete identification with the Divine will, a departure from the phenomenal world into Supreme is the final thing to be achieved.

Merits and Demerits of Traditional Systems

The highest perfection and preservation of physical form and life is one of the objects of physical nature. A greater enjoyment of the physical living is also included in that object. Hathayoga fulfills this object in an abundant measure. But, hathayoga is very laborious and difficult making a great demand on the time and energy of the individual. It also imposes a complete severance from the ordinary life of men. Though Yoga produces very extraordinary results, utilization of these results for the benefit of the world becomes impracticable or extremely restricted. Therefore, Sri Aurobindo says:

> "Hathayoga attains large results, but at an exorbitant price and to very little purpose".[4]

Rajayoga achieves a super-normal perfection and enlargement of capacities of mental life. As a result its ultimate aim is to realize not only subjective empire (*swarajya*), but also outward empire (*samrajya*), the control by subjective consciousness of its outer activities and environment. A weakness of the system is excessive reliance on abnormal states of trance. A certain aloofness from the physical life becomes inevitable. This prevents us to bring out mental and spiritual gains into the physical life which is our foundation. Since spiritual life is too much associated with the state of *samadhi*, it is impossible to make the spiritual life and its experiences fully active and utilizable in the waking state. Another difficulty is that it encourages to withdraw with higher plane exclusively and not descend into the whole existence and possess it.

Though, tantrayoga is world affirming unlike hathayoga and rajayoga and more comprehensive than either of them, it has also its own limitation. One of the serious drawbacks of this Yoga is that it consists of a very highly complicated process of purification and worship. Unless one is extremely alert, he is likely to miss essential spirit and get only peripheral advantages. Commenting on this Sri Aurobindo says, "Tantric Yoga largely lost its principle in its machinery and became a thing of formulae and occult mechanism still powerful when rightly used but fallen from the clarity of their original intention."[5]

The triple path regards man as an essentially a mental being and its capacity to relate individual to the Divine is based on the fact that mind is the most evolved part in human being. Generally speaking, the triple path is indifferent to mental and bodily perfection. Its whole emphasis is on purity as the condition of divine realization. Another defect is that though paths are parallel one of them is chosen as an exclusive approach to the Divine. Also the chosen one is treated as a system which cannot be reconciled with others. A third defect, common to the three systems, is that it leads away from world existence to an absorption in the supracosmic.

REFERENCES

1. Sri Aurobindo, *The Synthesis of Yoga*, Sri Aurobindo Ashram, Pondicherry, 1965, p. 27.
2. *S.Y.*, p. 493.
3. Sir John Woodroffe, *Shakti and Shakta*, Ganesh and Co., Madras, 1959, p. 579.
4. *S.Y.*, p. 29.
5. *Ibid.*, p. 36.

Chapter 2

The Gita's Synthesis of Works, Knowledge and Devotion

The Central Aim of the Gita

The Gita consists of 18 chapters. There is a tradition among scholars regarding the classification of the chapters into three broad divisions. The first division comprises of chapters 1 to 6; the second division chapters 7 to 12 and the last division chapters 13 to 18. It is further maintained that these divisions gradually unfold the central significance of the Gita. Sri Aurobindo says that the first six chapters of Gita are devoted to reconciling the paths of works and knowledge.

The words Sankhya and Yoga, as they are used in the Gita, stand respectively for knowledge and works. The word Sankhya stands for Yoga which proceeds by knowledge. It is by intellectual discrimination that it attains the vision and possession of the truth of our being.

The word Yoga refers to a method which proceeds by works the aim of which is to practice truth attained by knowledge. The Gita itself comes to our rescue in identifying the meaning of those terms Sankhya and Yoga. It says, "In this world twofold is the self application of the soul; That of Sankhya by the Yoga of knowledge, that of *Yogins* by the Yoga of works."[1] Speaking of the significance of the first six chapters Sri Aurobindo writes:

> The whole object of the first six chapters of the Gita is to synthetise in a large frame of Vedantic truth the two methods, ordinarily supposed to be diverse and even opposite, of the Sankhyas and the Yogins. The Sankhya is taken as the starting point and the basis; but it is from the beginning and with a progressively increasing emphasis permeated with the ideas the methods of Yoga and remoulded in its spirit. The practical difference, as it seems to have presented itself to the religious minds of that day, lay first in this that Sankhya proceeded by knowledge and through the Yoga of the intelligence, while Yoga proceeded by works and the transformation of the active consciousness.[2]

Though the first division aims to arrive at a synthesis of works and knowledge it does not fulfill all the conditions necessary for attaining its aim. As Sri Aurobindo points out the synthesis is carried to a certain level without the clear expression and decisive entrance of those ideas which when presented must enlarge and modify original idea of reconciliation. However, the chapters covered by this first division introduces a number of hints which in themselves are of capital importance. These hints are reserved for much larger treatment in the subsequent divisions. It is worth-while to quote here

Sri Aurobindo who brings home the value of first six chapters of the Gita in a beautiful manner.

> "If the Gita were not a great written scripture which must be carried out to its end, if it were actually a discourse by a living teacher to a disciple which could be resumed in good time, when the disciple was ready for further truth, and could conceive of his stopping here at the end of the sixth chapter and saying, "Work this out first, there is plenty for you to do to realize it and you have the largest possible basis; as difficulties arise, they will solve themselves or I will solve them for you. But at present live out what I have told you; work in this spirit."[3]

Chapters from seventh to twelfth come out with a comprehensive metaphysical account of the nature of the Divine Being. They synthetise knowledge and devotion on the metaphysical foundation. The third and the last division reaches a point of grand reconciliation of works, knowledge and devotion. Thus, the Gita may be looked upon as a work of synthesis of knowledge, works and devotion.

Karmayoga

Under normal circumstances *karma* begets *karma*. All *karma* is not only the expression of bondage but also a source of further bondage. As a yogic discipline *karma* is turned into a powerful means of not only dissolving the knots of bondage but also emerging into a life of freedom. What is it that, makes *karma* a means of liberation? The Gita points out that whether action is a source of bondage or not depends upon the attitude with which it is performed. There is no action which does not produce its consequence. Normally when we act we are motivated to act by the desire to enjoy the fruits of our action. It is this desire for fruits that makes an act as a source of bondage. In order to turn *karma* into a means of freedom we must change our attitude and never allow ourselves to be motivated by the fruits of our action. The Gita declares, "Thou hast a right to action, but only to action, never to its fruits; let not the fruits of thy works be thy motive, neither let there be in thee any attachment to inactivity."[4] But we should remember that to reject the fruits of action as the motivating factor is not to reject action itself. To emphasis the need to act in a new perspective the Gita says that, our concern is only for action and that action should never be given up. This is the significance of what it says elsewhere, "Action is greater than inaction."[5] The two-fold effects of *karma* performed in this new perspective is indicated by the Gita; first, it dissolves the knots of bondage and second, it leads to the higher life of freedom. The Gita says that, works done without attachment makes self purification possible;[6] in another place it says that, by doing works without attachment man attains to the highest.[7] The definition of Yoga as skill in works[8] must be understood only in this light; works done in the ordinary manner lead to bondage, whereas works performed in the yogic spirit lead to freedom.

Jnanayoga

The consciousness of the ordinary man is completely obscured in the functions of his senses. The senses are directed towards material objects. Desire is the effect of this attachment; distress, passion and anger are effects of desire. With the result the consciousness is completely obscured and its natural quality of discrimination and will has no opportunity to assert itself. In the words of Sri

Aurobindo, "We become passion, wrath, grief and cease to be self and intelligence and will."[9] It is by self-control that the consciousness identified with the senses and the sense-objects, must be restored. The Gita describes how the loss of true consciousness leads to a series of effects resulting in the loss of person himself. It says, "In him whose mind dwells on the objects of sense with absorbing interest, attachment to them is formed; from attachment arises desire; from desire anger comes forth. Anger leads to bewilderment; from bewilderment comes loss of memory; and by that intelligence is destroyed; from destruction of intelligence he perishes."[10] The Gita describes the man of true knowledge as one who is of settled understanding. He is free from desire wrath, liking and fear.[11] It adds that he is like a tortoise. As the tortoise draws his limbs into the shell, so he draws away the senses from the object of sense and sits firmly founded in wisdom.[12] The effort to conquer the senses and to keep them always under control is very difficult even for the sages. "Even the mind of the wise man who labours for perfection is carried away by vehement insistence of the senses."[13] However, it does not mean that the conquest of the senses is impossible. Rather it is the only way by which we have to recover our true consciousness. The Gita says, "Having brought all senses under control, he must sit firm in yoga; for whose senses are mastered, of him the consciousness is firmly established."[14] He who is in possession of knowledge is completely free from all works. In Gita's language all works are turned to ashes by the fire of knowledge.[15] Such a knowledge is declared to be so great that nothing in this world is equal to it in purity.[16] On attainment of knowledge one's ordinary self is extinguished in Brahman.[17] Knowledge leads to Supreme peace.[18]

Bhaktiyoga

Like thought and will emotions also could be a powerful means of liberation. Normally, emotions are directed towards external objects and therefore, becomes sources of bondage. When emotions are redirected towards God, they elevate man to a higher life of freedom. All pain and suffering acquire new significance and cease to create bewilderment. Of all the emotions those of love and self-giving are the most powerful. He who loves the divine and gives himself entirely to the object of his love becomes a true devotee. The Gita describes the nature of the devotee as one who is steadfast in spiritual endeavour and always in adoration of the Lord and bowing down with devotion.[19] The teacher of the Gita declares that, he spontaneously brings every good to the devotee who worships him as the whole object of thought and devotion. The Gita says, "To those men who worship Me making Me alone the whole object of their thought, to those constantly in yoga with Me, I spontaneously bring every good".[20] The teacher of the Gita promises that he who loves him gets eternal peace and never perishes. "This is my word of promise, that he who loves me shall not perish."[21]

Works and Knowledge

The Gita seems to advocate two opposite views regarding works and knowledge. In one place it says that, works are important and should not be given up.[22] In another place it says that, works are far inferior to knowledge.[23] Therefore, Arjuna is asking "If thou holdest knowledge to be greater than works, O Janardana why then does thou, O Keshava, appoint me to a terrible work? Thou seemest to bewilder my intelligence with a confused and mingled speech; tell me then decisively that one thing by which I may attain to my soul's weal."[24] The Gita also gives the impression that knowledge is the only thing desirable in the world[25] and makes all works impossible.[26] It says that for he who has achieved knowledge there exists no work that needs to be done.[27] The Gita clarifies that both works and knowledge are important. It says "Children speak of Sankhya (knowledge) and Yoga (works) apart from each other, not the wise; if a man applies himself integrally to one, he gets the fruits of both. The status which is attained by the Sankhya (knowledge), to that of men of the Yoga (works) also arrive; who seeks Sankhya (knowledge) and Yoga (works) as one, he sees."[28] Works done without attachment leads to self-purification and finally knowledge of Brahman.[29] The rise of knowledge destroys works performed out of ignorance, works motivated by desire, but it does not destroy works as such, for works are done by nature.[30] The works are said to be reposed on Brahman.[31] In fact, works become efficient when they are performed in the light of knowledge.[32] In this context, the distinction is made between *karma* and *kartavyamkarma* or *niyatamkarma*. *Karma* is what is generated by desire, whereas *kartavyamkarma* or *niyatamkarma* is impelled and regulated by the will of the Divine. Therefore, the latter kind of action is not opposed to knowledge. Rather knowledge supports and makes possible those *karmas*. Gita very clearly says that renunciation of *niyatamkarma* is improper.

Knowledge and Devotion

Absolute control of the senses is the necessary prerequisite to knowledge. However, the Gita adds that another condition needs to be fulfilled in order to be firmly established in knowledge. "Having brought all the senses under control, he must sit firm in Yoga wholly given up to Me."[33] Commenting on the significance of the verse Sri Aurobindo writes:

> This (to be firmly established in intelligence or knowledge) cannot be done perfectly by the act of the intelligence itself, by a merely mental self-discipline; it can only be done by Yoga with something which is higher than itself and in which calm and self-mastery are inherent. And this Yoga can only arrive at its success by devoting, by consecrating, by giving up the whole self to the Divine, "to Me", says Krishna; for the Liberator is within us, but it is not our mind, nor our intelligence nor our personal will, .. they are only instruments. It is the Lord in whom, as we are told in the end, we have utterly to take refuge. And for that we must at first make him the object of our whole being and keep in soul-contact with him. This is the sense of the phrase "he must sit firm in Yoga, wholly given up to me"; but as yet it is the merest passing hint after the manner of the Gita, three words only which contain in seed the whole gist of the highest secret yet to be developed, *yukta asita matparah.*[34]

It is therefore the evident that without devotion to Divine it is impossible to be firmly established in knowledge. But then why is devotion necessary? The answer to this question lies in grasping the true significance of the word "Me" which occurs in the verse quoted above.[35] The word "Me" represents a fundamental metaphysical truth upon which the whole teaching of the Gita is founded.

In the seventh chapter of the Gita what was mentioned as the passing hint in the previous chapters, particularly in the second, is developed in reference to the distinction between the lower and the higher nature of the Divine. The idea is further taken up and fully developed in the 15th chapter, where the concept of "Purushottama" is presented. The Divine is both immutable and mutable, *akshara purusha* and *kshara purusha*. And yet it is other because it is more and greater than either of these opposites. As it exceeds both it is called Purushottama. It is the metaphysical basis of reconciliation of works and knowledge. By knowledge one enters into the immutable aspect of the Divine. But unless one raises into the higher nature of the Divine, *paraprakriti*, one is not really free to act without being bound by works. It must be noted here that the higher nature and "Purushottama" are identical. Verse six in chapter seven indicates their identity. It is therefore clear that "Purushottama" is the integral divine to whom immutability and mutability are the two aspects. This is the meaning of the word "Me" which occurs in the second chapter. In the same sense the word is used in subsequent chapters also.

When the Gita says that he who has brought the senses under control must be firmly established in knowledge wholly given up to "Me", means two things: (1) he must reach Purushottama which represents the supreme unity of action and inaction; (2) and the way to reach "Purushottama" is devotion and self-surrender. In order to be free from works and perform them without being bound by their effects, knowledge is the essential step. But knowledge alone is not sufficient. It must culminate in devotion so that knowledge becomes a natural basis of *kartavyamkarma* or *niyatamkarma*. He who devotes himself to the integral divine with knowledge as his basis, is regarded as the best devotee. The teacher of the Gita says, such a person loves Him perfectly and is His beloved.[36]

Works, Knowledge and Devotion

In chapter nine of the Gita we come across a number of verses which clearly indicate that Purushottama is the meeting ground of the three yogas: works, knowledge and devotion. The teacher of the Gita says, "Whatever thou doest, whateve. thou enjoyest whatever thou sacrificest, whatever thou givest, whatever energy of *tapasya*, of the soul's will or effort, thou puttest forth, make it an offering unto Me."[37] Here works are elevated to the highest level of devotion as they are done as an integral offering to the Divine. In the next verse he says, "thy soul in union with the Divine through renunciation thou shall become free and attain to me."[38] Here knowledge is uplifted to the level of attaining integral union with Divine to whom all works have become devoted offerings. The following verse, "Those who turn to Me with love and devotion, they are in Me and I also in them."[39] Here devotion is upgraded into the highest ecstasy of union supported by integral knowledge and surrender of works. Thus, while devotion takes knowledge and works to the highest level of union and surrender, knowledge and works elevate devotion itself to the highest point of ecstasy of union and surrender.

The Limitation of the Gita's Synthesis

According to Sri Aurobindo's interpretation of Gita, the paths of works, knowledge and devotion are not exclusive. By a monumental synthesis of these three the Gita proposes to raise the whole consciousness of man to the Divine. A total turning of whole human being through will, knowledge and love leads to realizing the integrality of the Divine and an integral self-fulfillment. The Gita very clearly shows how the three lines intertwine and interfuse as they proceed towards the goal. However, there are two things to which the Gita does not seem to give careful consideration: (1) "The Gita starts with Sankhyayoga, that is to say, with a separation between Purusha and Prakriti through the instrumentality of the Buddhi, the most enlightened part of the human mind; but it seems to be rather a poor and precarious beginning for the realization of such a stupendously dynamic aim; for the Buddhi is, after all, a tool of the lower nature, and cannot be a safe guide in such an adventure"[40], (2) "The end of the Gita's synthetic yoga has been left wrapped in a mysterious hint of a total divine living for man; but the *uttamam rahasyam,* the supreme mystery, has nowhere been resolved and outlined before the gaze of the spiritual seeker. A living in the Divine, a constant, blissful and dynamic living in the Purushottama, emerges, as the *grand finale* of the synthetic Yoga of the Gita; but by what definite culminating steps will this consummation be attained, by what process of transmutation and transfiguration of this base metal of human nature, and what will be the status and active poise of the individual in that victorious apotheosis, and the purpose and influence of his presence in the world, have been left to be worked out in the experience of the sadhaka."[41] For a sadhaka whose aim is to attain integral perfection, perfection of being and nature, the synthesis offered by the Gita is sufficient to undertake the venture, but not sufficient to go through the adventure.

REFERENCES

1. *The Bhagavad Gita,* 3-3.
2. Sri Aurobindo, *Essays on the Gita,* Sri Aurobindo Ashram, Pondicherry, 1970, p. 75.
3. *E.G.,* p. 236.
4. *B.G.,* pp. 2-47.

5. *Ibid.*, pp. 3-8.
6. *Ibid.*, pp. 5-11.
7. *Ibid.*, pp. 3-19.
8. *Ibid.*, pp. 2-50.
9. *E.G.*, p. 94.
10. *B.G.*, pp. 2-62, 63.
11. *Ibid.*, pp. 2-56.
12. *Ibid.*, pp. 2-58.
13. *Ibid.*, pp. 2-60.
14. *Ibid.*, pp. 2-61.
15. *Ibid.*, pp. 4-37.
16. *Ibid.*, pp. 4-38.
17. *Ibid.*, pp. 2-72.
18. *Ibid.*, pp. 4-39.
19. *Ibid.*, pp. 9-14.
20. *Ibid.*, pp. 9-22.
21. *Ibid.*, pp. 9-31.
22. *Ibid.*, pp. 3-8.
23. *Ibid.*, pp. 2-49.
24. *Ibid.*, pp. 3-1, 2.
25. *Ibid.*, pp. 4-38.
26. *Ibid.*, pp. 4-37.
27. *Ibid.*, pp. 3-17.
28. *Ibid.*, pp. 5-4, 5.
29. *Ibid.*, pp. 5-11, 12.
30. *Ibid.*, pp. 5-14.
31. *Ibid.*, pp. 5-10.
32. *Ibid.*, pp. 2-50.

33. *Ibid.*, pp. 2-61.
34. *E.G.*, p. 94.
35. *B.G.*, pp. 2-61.
36. *Ibid.*, pp. 7-17.
37. *Ibid.*, pp. 9-27.
38. *Ibid.*, pp. 9-28.
39. *Ibid.*, pp. 9-29.
40. Rishabhchand, *The Integral Yoga of Sri Aurobindo,* Sri Aurobindo Ashram, Pondicherry, 1959, p. 28.
41. *Ibid.*, pp. 28-29.

CHAPTER 3

THE IDEAL OF INTEGRAL PERFECTION AND A SYNTHESIS OF TRADITIONAL SYSTEMS

The Integral Ideal

Yoga is a practical means to realize the ideal formulated by metaphysical enquiry. The metaphysics of Sri Aurobindo affirms that, integral perfection is the ultimate goal to be achieved. Since, it regards man as a divine spiritual being involved in mind, life and body, its goal is liberation and perfection of his divine nature. The Yoga, based on this ideal has two significant aspects; (1) It seeks to make an inner living in the perfectly developed spiritual being, a constant intrinsic living, and (2) Its outward human expression is the spiritualized action of mind, life and body. Apart from these, it goes beyond mind to a supramental knowledge, will, sense feeling, intuition and vital and physical action. They constitute the native working of the spiritual being. It accepts human life with a view to elevate it to a far higher level where the whole life is aware of its divine source and feels in each action of knowledge, of will, of feeling, sense and body, the divine impulse. It does not reject anything that is essential in earthly life. On the contrary it tries to enlarge it and finds its true meaning and value. Therefore a Yoga committed to such a larger aim must be in its nature and effectively comprehensive and integral.

An Integral Yoga as outlined above must be in a position to arrive at a synthesis of the leading systems of Yoga. To combine them without discrimination will not lead to a synthesis. It can only create confusion. Nor is synthesis achieved by a successive practice of each of them, for our limited energy and short span of life do not permit such an attempt. It is really a cumbrous process which implies waste of labour and time. In fact, Ramakrishna paramahamsa attempted a synthesis of the major systems of Yoga and succeeded in his endeavour. He is an extraordinary man and his example cannot be generalized. Commenting on the synthetic work of Ramakrishna Paramahamsa, Sri Aurobindo writes:

> "In the life of Ramakrishna Paramahamsa, we see a colossal spiritual capacity, first driving straight to the divine realization, taking, as it were, the kingdom of heaven by violence, and then seizing upon one Yogic method after another and extracting the substance out of it with an incredible rapidity, always to return to the heart of the whole matter, the realization and possession of God by the power of love, by the extension of inborn spirituality into various experience and by the spontaneous play of an intuitive knowledge. Such an example cannot be generalized".[1]

Therefore, a synthesis of the traditional systems

cannot be arrived at either by combination in mass or by successive practice. Unless the following conditions are fulfilled a real synthesis cannot be achieved: (1) The forms and the outsides of the spiritual disciplines must be set aside, (2) Some central principle common to all systems should become fundamental basis, and (3) Some central dynamic force common to all systems must have the capacity to organize the natural selection and combination of the various elements and utilities.

So far, we have outlined the conditions under which different systems can be harmonized. Now we have to mention some of the qualities that characterize the working of a synthetic Yoga.

1. A synthetic Yoga does not act according to a fixed system and succession as found in the traditional schools of Yoga. Its working is free, scattered and yet gradually intensive depending upon the temperament of the individual.

2. It accepts our nature as it is and compels it to undergo a divine change. It discovers that all lower forms are just deformations of the higher. We are reminded of the words of Vedic *rishis* who say that Gods are fashioned by human forefathers even as a smith forges the crude material in his smithy.

3. It takes every experience and outer contact with the world and considers them very useful for the work. It looks upon every inner experience as a step on the path to perfection.

The Synthesis of the Systems

An examination of the traditional systems of Yoga reveals that each Yoga has its own characteristic instrument and this determines the nature of its essential process. The hathayogic process is psycho-physical whereas the rajayogic process is mental and psychic. The path of knowledge is spiritual and cognitive; the path of devotion is spiritual, emotional and aesthetic; the way of works is spiritual and dynamic by action. Each Yoga is guided by its own characteristic power. And all power is ultimately one soul-power. In the ordinary workings of life, body and mind the soul-power is below the surface. When the surface functions are brought under control, the hidden soul-power emerges and reveals its essential unity. Because soul-power is all-power it is likely to be attended by the other results characteristic of other paths even though it normally associated as a result of one particular path. This suggests the possibility of a synthetic Yoga.

The synthetic Yoga will be essentially a yoga of self-surrender. It will be a giving up of human being to the being, consciousness, power and delight of the Divine. But at the same time its object will be more comprehensive and complete. Normally the initial purpose of the traditional systems in the liberation of the soul from its present limitation and ignorance. Liberation is not a mere deliverance from ignorance and limitation; it is also an entry into spiritual being, a union with the highest Self and God. This is the goal and final object of all traditional systems. If there is any place for enjoyment it is either in a dissolution of the individual in the transcendent self or on a higher plane in another existence. But the Tantric system is an exception in which the final goal of liberation permits a full perfection and enjoyment of the spiritual power in the world. The synthetic yoga like the Tantric system, will envisage the possibility of spiritual enjoyment of the universe without prejudice to the need for liberation. The synthetic Yoga will be even more progressive than the Tantric system. The liberated individual, in the wider view of the synthetic Yoga, will be a channel for pouring the divine riches upon the human race. Sri Aurobindo describes how the Integral Yoga is more comprehensive than the Tantric system:

> The human soul's individual liberation and enjoyment of union with the Divine in spiritual being, consciousness and delight must always be the first object of the Yoga; its free enjoyment of the cosmic unity of the Divine becomes a second object; but out of that a third appears, the effectuation of the meaning of the divine unity with all beings by a sympathy and participation in the spiritual purpose of the Divine in humanity. The individual Yoga then turns from its separateness and becomes a part of the collective Yoga of the divine Nature in the human race. The liberated individual being, united with the Divine in self and spirit, becomes in his natural being a self-perfecting instrument for the perfect outflowering of the Divine in humanity.[2]

Thus, the synthetic Yoga will offer itself as a synthesis at three levels: (1) At the first level, it is the synthesis of the individual soul with the Supreme Being; (2) at the second level, it is a synthesis of soul and nature in the individual; and (3) at the third level, it is a synthesis of the individual man and the society.

REFERENCES

1. *S.Y.*, p. 34.
2. *Ibid.*, p. 573.

Part - III

Philosophical Background of Integral Yoga

CHAPTER 4

THE METAPHYSICAL BASIS OF INTEGRAL YOGA

Dualism and its Solution

A theory which says that, the world is constituted of two fundamental realities goes by the name dualism. It affirms not only the existence of two fundamental realities but also a relation of mutual exclusion and contradiction. A metaphysical theory of dualism says that, *purusha* and *prakriti* are the two ultimate realities of the world. While *purusha* is the luminous spirit, *prakriti* is the mechanically active energy. They are so fundamentally different that they have nothing in common. From one point of view, Sankara also may be said to have offered the dualism of the inactive Brahman and the ever changing Maya. Brahman is nameless and formless, whereas Maya is the source of names and forms. They are fundamentally disparate and irreconciliable entities. But dualism always tends to resolve its inherent contradiction by subordinating one of the terms to the other. Sankhya overcomes the contradiction by dissolving *prakriti* into the immutable repose of *purusha*. Sankara gets over the difficulty by a dissolution of Maya into Brahman. It has been inevitable result of dualism for the human mind cannot rest satisfied with any kind of contradiction. When talking about "The Realistic Dualism", Dr. Radhakrishnan says, it "is the result of a false metaphysics".[1]

The Statement of Materialism

Both materialism and asceticism have come into existence as a result of an attempt to overcome the contradiction between Matter and Spirit. Materialism says that Matter alone is real and spirit is dismissed as the dream of the mind or an abstraction of the rational faculty. The materialist premise is that the material world is the only thing about which we can be certain. Anything that is considered to lie beyond the material world is dismissed as wholly unknowable. The reality of Matter is affirmed by the physical senses. Since they are unable to perceive anything immaterial or not organized as gross matter, it presumed that the supraphysical is unreal.

The Limitation and Value of Materialism

When materialism concludes that the supraphysical is unknowable, it fails to understand that its conclusion is valid only relatively. The supraphysical may be unknowable by thought, but not unknowable by a supreme effort of consciousness. The human mind is certainly a higher faculty but not the highest. The supraphysical is knowable by faculties other than the mental. Sri Aurobindo says that, as a rule, all things in the universe that are considered to be unknowable at present pre-suppose corresponding faculties that somewhere exist in man in an undeveloped form and are capable of development.

Materialism is not without its value. It teaches that nothing is true unless it proves itself to be beyond doubt. A rational enquiry can lead to fruitful knowledge only when it passes through an initial stage of agnosticism. In the absence of agnosticism the intellect is not fully qualified to enter any field of knowledge, for it is likely to lend itself to perilous distortion and misleading imaginations. A fully disciplined intellect alone can effectively deal with the materials that pour into our mind when super sensible faculties come into operation. A fully trained intellect alone has the capacity to correct the errors in knowledge, because nothing short of such a faculty can maintain a proper relationship to sensible facts and concrete realities of the physical world. It is a fact that in proportion to the extent and certainty of our knowledge of the physical world, our foundation of higher knowledge becomes wider and surer. Sri Aurobindo says:

> The touch of Earth is always reinvigorating to the son of Earth, even when he seeks a supraphysical Knowledge. It may even be said that the supraphysical can only be really mastered in its fullness-to its heights we can always reach — when we keep our feet firmly on the physical. "Earth is His footing" says the Upanishad whenever it images the Self that manifests in the universe.[2]

The Statement of Asceticism

The ascetic fixes his attention on the reality of spirit which is beyond the material world and refuses to recognise the truth of the material world. He finds in the spirit complete freedom from change, birth and death. And the world which contradicts the spiritual freedom is dismissed as the abstraction of the mind. When the mind passes suddenly into the realm of spirit, without intermediate transitions, receives a sense of unreality of the world and the sole reality of the spirit. This is parallel to the position of the materialist. In point of fact, the refusal of the ascetic to recognise the reality of the world is more complete, more final and more perilous in its effects.

The Limitation and Value of Asceticism

Indian cultural history bears witness to the fact how far asceticism held its sway on the Indian mind. The great consensus was that not in world of dualities could there be "Our kingdom of heaven, but beyond, whether in the joys of the eternal Vrindavan or the high beatitude of Brahmaloka beyond all manifestations in some ineffable Nirvana".[3] This one sidedness is due to the failing of vital energy of the Indian race which by its many sided contribution to human effort and knowledge arrived at a point of complete exhaustion. Nevertheless, asceticism has played a significant role in the development of human perfection. But for it, it would have been impossible for the race to come out of the hold of animalism. Sri Aurobindo writes:

> The ascetic spirit is an indispensable element in human perfection and even its separate affirmation cannot be avoided so long as the race has not at the other end liberated its intellect and its vital habits from subjection to an always insistent animalism.[4]

Materialism and Asceticism

Materialism and asceticism respectively represent the attitudes of two different cultures, the European and the Indian. In Europe, materialism symbolizes the fullness of riches and triumphant mastery of the world's powers and possessions. Likewise asceticism signifies the great heaping up of the treasures of the spirit. Representing as they do two different extremes, materialism led towards a great bankruptcy of life, while asceticism progressed towards an equal bankruptcy in the things of the spirit.

Materialism holds that because the corporal organs do not have access to the supraphysical realities, the supraphysical has to be dismissed as unreal. As we have pointed out earlier, if the corporal organs are incapable of dealing with the supraphysical they give place to appropriate supraphysical faculties which can take cognizance of that reality. Once the higher faculties emerge in us we begin to see the deeper truths of the material world. We may discover that matter itself is a self-involution of consciousness in form and a self-evolution out of form, so as to actualize some mighty possibility in the universe which it has created. So what is required to understand the material world in proper perspective is an extension of consciousness into the cosmic level. One realizes that the consciousness has the greater reality than the physical world. The consciousness is real in itself and real in its effects and works. It is real to the world and the world is real to it. The world is real because it exists only in consciousness. It is not necessary now to regard spirit or matter as unreal in order to affirm the reality of the one or the other. They do not exclude each other, rather they become one. Sri Aurobindo writes:

> "If Matter is one end, Spirit is the other. The two are one. Spirit is the soul and reality of that which we sense as Matter; Matter is a form and body of that which we realize as Spirit".[5]

Brahman as the Indeterminable Reality

We have shown that in the cosmic consciousness matter becomes real to the spirit and spirit becomes real to matter. They are reconciled in the context of a spiritual perception which reveals to the observing consciousness that they admit each other. But it is necessary to show by a logical analysis of the concepts of Brahman and matter that they are not mutually exclusive or contradictory.

Brahman is said to be indefinable, infinite, timeless and spaceless existence. It means that Brahman is without definitions, without limitations, without spacial and temporal distinctions. It does not mean that Brahman is the opposite of the definable, the finite, the temporal and the spacial. When we say that, Brahman is without definitions etc., "We mean that it exceeds them, that it is something into which they pass in such a way as to cease to be what we call form, quality, quantity and out of which they emerge as form quality and quantity in the movement".[6] The Taittiriya Upanishad says that, out of the Non-Being, Being appeared (2-7). If the Non-Being is a negation of the Being, then the Being cannot appear out of it. Since the Being is born out of the Non-Being, the Non-Being cannot be a negative conception. Sri Aurobindo explains the meaning of the Non-Being:

> We give the name of Non-Being to a contrary affirmation of Its freedom from all cosmic existence, freedom, that is to say, from all positive terms of actual existence which consciousness in the universe

> can formulate to itself, even from the most abstract, even from the most transcendent. It does not deny them as a real expression of Itself, but It denies Its limitation by all expression or any expression whatsoever.[7]

Brahman is indeterminable not in the sense that it is incapable of self-determination but in the sense that it cannot be limited by any determination or any sum of possible determinations.

The Infinite Power of Brahman

Brahman is not only an infinite Being but also an infinite power. It is not only an eternal repose and quiescence but eternal action and creation. Its action is an action in itself, a creation out of its own self, eternal and infinite, for there is nothing out of which it can create. Any basis of creation, which seems to be other than itself must be still really in itself and of itself. It cannot be something foreign to its existence. We cannot suppose that Brahman is compelled by something outside or other than itself, since no such thing exists. Nor is it possible to suppose that Brahman submits unwillingly to something partial within itself which is hostile to its whole being, because it erects a contradiction of Brahman and the creative power which is other than Brahman. All erection or becoming is nothing but self-manifestation of Brahman. Sri Aurobindo writes:

> What it produces is itself and can be nothing other than itself; it is working out a play, a rhythm, a development of its own existence, force of consciousness and delight of being. Therefore whatever comes into the world, seeks nothing but this, to be, to arrive at the intended form, to enlarge

> its self-existence in that form, to develop, manifest, increase, realize infinitely the consciousness and the power that is in it, to have the delight of coming into manifestation, the delight of the form of being, the delight of the rhythm of consciousness, the delight of the play of force and to aggrandise and perfect that delight by whatever means is possible, in whatever direction, through whatever idea of itself may be suggested to it by the Existence, the Conscious — Force, the Delight active within its deepest being.[8]

We have found that all things are Brahman, self-manifestation of Existence, Conscious-Force and Delight. But this does not explain the process by which Brahman turned itself into this phenomenal world. There must be a process, a law that could explain how the cosmic manifestation proceeds out of Brahman. There must be a self-determining power in the universal consciousness of Brahman and a capacity in Brahman's existence to perceive a certain truth in itself and direct its force of creation along the line of that truth. Brahman is infinite consciousness and it can produce only infinite results through its infinite action. Its manifestation can only be infinity of figures without fixed order or relation. In order to fix determined relation and prevent the forces of confusion from interfering with the process of ordered creation, a selective faculty of knowledge is necessary. It is in this aspect that the Isha Upanishad describes Brahman as the Infinite Seer and Thinker[8]. This power of self-limitation is necessarily inherent in the infinite Brahman, otherwise it would not be infinite. To quote Sri Aurobindo:

> The Infinite would not be the Infinite if it could not assume a manifold finiteness; the Absolute would not be the Absolute if it were denied in

knowledge and power and will and manifestation of being a boundless capacity of self-determination.[9]

This power is referred to as *Maya* by the Vedic seers. The term in its original sense meant a comprehending and containing consciousness capable of embracing, measuring and limiting. It denotes that which outlines, measures out, moulds forms in the formless, geometrises and makes measurable the limitless. Only later the word came to acquire a sense of cunning, fraud or illusion. This power is also referred to as the fourth Name of the Nameless, *turiyasvid*. It is called the fourth because the infinite Brahman is referred by three other names, Existence, Consciousness and Bliss. Sri Aurobindo employs the word 'Supermind' to denote this power.

The Three Essential Powers of Brahman

Like the being of Brahman its power of being is absolutely free. Sri Aurobindo points out that there are three essential powers of Brahman to show how the law of illimitable freedom works in the context of its consciousness-force. The three essential powers are:

(a) The 'power of self-variation'[10],

(b) The 'power of self-limitation'[11], and

(c) The 'power of self-absorption'.[12]

(a) The Power of Self-Variation is natural to a consciousness, that is, infinite. It cannot be bound to a finite restriction of itself or to one state or law of its action. It can be many things simultaneously without any difficulty. It can be one but innumerably manifold. It can put many states of consciousness at a time, without ceasing to be the same consciousness-force forever. This power of Brahman is known as the power of self-variation.

(b) The Power of Self-Limitation or secondary self-formation is a power of Brahman by which it is able to impose limitations on itself. This power of self-limitation has two manifestations: (1) the individual self-limitation, and (2) the cosmic self-limitation. The power of individual self-limitation means the capacity of Brahman to express itself in the form of individual beings or souls. The power of cosmic-limitation means the capacity of Brahman which is responsible for the existence and working of the universe. The power of self-limitation has also the capacity to put forth some powers like Mind, Life and Matter. This power of self-limitation of the infinite and illimitable consciousness appears contradictory to our normal reason. But the logic of the infinite[13] shows that this is also one of its powers.

(c) The Power of Self-Absorption has two expressions: Superconscience and Inconscience. In the state of Superconscience the self-absorption takes place without abolishing self-awareness, but in the state of Inconscience there is no self-awareness. It is out of the Inconscient that an ordered world is created. The states of the Superconscient and the Inconscient are due to a total self-absorption of the Infinite Consciousness. There is also partial self-absorption of the Infinite Consciousness confined to a particular status such as of Mind, Life and Matter.

Mind, Life and Matter

The principles of Mind, Life and Matter are nothing but the self-limited and self-concentrated forms of Brahman. Though they appear to be different from Brahman, really they are one with Brahman. By its very nature Mind cuts and divides the integral whole. It deals with things as if they were separate things in themselves and not as aspects of a whole. Even if it knows that they are not things in themselves, it can subject them to its own characteristic activity and deals with them as if they were things in themselves. All its operative powers like conception, perception, sensation and other dealings of creative thought are conditioned by this essential characteristic of Mind. It is to translate always infinity into the terms of the finite.

When the apprehending power of Supermind introduces a process of variation into the forms that are bound by an indivisible relationship in order to carry the process of division to a further point, the Mind is used as a subordinate action of the infinite knowledge, a definition of things subordinate to its awareness of infinity. We may therefore say that Mind is the final operation of the apprehending power of the Supermind. As a subordinate power of Supermind, Mind serves only to create a certain form of separation necessary in the process of manifestation of the world. There is no falsification or distortion but only an extension of the apprehending element in the Divine consciousness. To quote Sri Aurobindo:

> And when the action of the mind is consciously subordinate to this knowledge of the supermind, the truth of the process is known to it also and not at all ignored: there is no real division but only an infinitely multiple concentration into forms of being and into arrangements of the relation of those forms of being to each other in which division is a subordinate appearance of the whole process necessary to their spatial and temporal play.[14]

Life according to Sri Aurobindo, "is a form of the one cosmic Energy, a dynamic movement or current of it positive and negative, a constant act or play of the Force which builds up forms, energies them by a continual stream of stimulation and maintains them by an unceasing process of disintegration and renewal of their substance".[15] It brings a form into existence and again reduces it to non-existence. So disintegration of substance and renewal of substance, are the process of life. Death also is a process of life. Nothing in life that is manifested perishes. "All renews itself, nothing perishes"[16], says Sri Aurobindo. Death is a rapid disintegration subservient to life's necessity of change and variation of formal experience. When a physical form ceases, its material is broken up to serve as material for other forms of life. Just as Mind is only a final operation of the supermind, so also Life is only a final operation of the consciousness-force of which Supermind is the creative agent. Sri Aurobindo points out that though Life has its source in the Divine, it works out from the stand point of division created by Mind. Sri Aurobindo observes:

> As Mind is the finial individualizing operation of the all-comprehending and all-apprehending Supermind... so Life is the final operation by which the Force of Conscious-Being acting through the all-possessing and all-creative Will of the universal Supermind maintains and energies, constitutes and reconstitutes individual forms and acts in them as the basis of all the activities of the soul thus embodied. Life is the energy of the Divine continually generating itself in forms as in a dynamo and not only playing with the outgoing battery of its shocks on surrounding forms of things but receiving itself the incoming shocks of all life around as they pour in upon and penetrate the form from outside, from the environing universe.[17]

Just as Mind as a subordinate term of the Supermind supports an infinitely multiple concentration in forms of being and arranges the relations of those forms to each other, so also Life supplies the energy to all forms and establishes inter-change of energy between forms. As mind does not introduce a real division between forms, Life does not allow real opposition in the inter-change of energies between forms. What Mind does from its point of view of variation, Life translates it in terms of its principle of distribution of energy.

According to Sri Aurobindo, "Matter, like Mind and Life, is still Being or Brahman in its self-creative action. It is a form of the force of Conscious Being, a form given by Mind and realized by Life".[18] Therefore, Matter is a form of Spirit and they are not opposed to each other. The consciousness in matter is concealed. In its original form, it is the unatomic substance of conscious-being. It represents the Divine substance turned into a multiplicity of atomic beings. Like Mind and Life, it is a subordinate principle of infinite Existence. Sri Aurobindo says:

> As Mind is only a final action of Supermind in the descent towards creation and Life an action of Conscious-Force working in the conditions of the Ignorance created by this descent of Mind, so Matter, as we know it, is only the final form taken by conscious-being as the result of that working.[19]

The process of creation of the world out of the pure infinite substance of Brahman requires a selective process based on comprehending as well as apprehending knowledge. Through this process, the divine multiplicity comes into existence. But this principle has to be carried to its extreme potential by separativeness and division. Mind as a power of delimitation is commissioned to accomplish this aim with Life and Matter as its instruments. While Mind creates the idea of divided forms, Life transforms this idea by the principle of interchange of energy in forms. There is one more step which is necessary to complete the process initiated by Mind. The idea fixed by Mind must be given a gross and material form. This is achieved by Matter which represents atomic division and aggregation of substance.

Involution

As long as Mind has not separated itself from the action of supermind, as long as it is conscious of the fact that as an instrument of the supermind, its work is to hold forms apart from each other by a purely formal delimitation of their activity, the principle of separation has not been carried to its farthest limit. Therefore a new action of conscious force becomes necessary. A helplessly limited Mind as opposed to the freely limiting Mind is to be created now. When Mind separates itself from the action of the Supermind by an exclusive concentration of consciousness, it becomes subject to its own play and is no longer master of its own action. Now Mind perceives only the particular and not the universal. It views every phenomenon as a thing in itself and cannot possess the truth of oneness. It is at this point that Ignorance comes into play. Ignorance intervenes only when the creation of the world requires the help of an effective principle of separation. It should be noted that by itself the principle of separation does not belong to the power of Ignorance. In the absence of Ignorance manifestation of the world and separation of forms are conceivable. Only when a particular mode of action on the part of the principle of separation becomes necessary, it beings to work as a principle of Ignorance. Mind is separated on account of self-concentration or self-absorption of conscious force from its spiritual and supramental basis and hence is ignorant of reality. Speaking about the origin of ignorance, Sri Aurobindo says:

> The origin of the Ignorance must then be sought for in some self-absorbed concentration of Tapas, of Conscious-Force in action on a separate movement of the Force; to us this takes the appearance of mind identifying itself with the separate movement and identifying itself also in the movement separately with each of the forms resulting from it.[20]

The divided and the dividing Mind depieces and aggregates "*ad infinitum*". As an instrument of the Infinite, its action knows no end. It not only divides, but also aggregates. Both division and aggregation are the deformed conditions of the comprehending and the apprehending actions of the Supermind. The exclusive concentration on the idea of division in Mind becomes effective when Mind concentrates exclusively on Life and Matter, successively. As a result, the idea of separation of forms becomes a phenomenal reality supported by Life and Matter. When the exclusive concentration on the principle of separation reaches the level of Matter, Matter disappears into what Sri Aurobindo calls Inconscience. "This is the last stage of the decent of consciousness, an abysmal sleep, a fathomless trance of consciousness which is the profound basis of the action of material Nature".[21] Thus, there is a series of involutions, the involution of Mind in Life, of Life in Matter and of Matter into Inconscience. Sri Aurobindo says that this is the inevitable outcome of the principle of separation taken to its farthest limit. He writes:

> If each principle loosed into action must follow

its independent line and carry out its complete consequences, the principle of separation must also be allowed its complete course and arrive at its absolute consequence; this is the inevitable descent, *facilis descensus*, which Consciousness, once it admits the separative principle, follows till it enters by obscuring infinitesimal fragmentation, *tucchyena*, into the material Inconscience, — the Inconscient Ocean of the Rig Veda.[22]

Evolution

The Inconscience represents the all-conscious Brahman completely overcome by the infinitely divided substance of Matter. Though, a physical basis for infinite variation of one Being is achieved by process of involution of which the appearance of the Inconscience is the final outcome, the involved action of the Inconscience is only a temporary mode of action. This can be abolished once the purpose is served. Therefore, corresponding to different stage of involution, a series of evolution takes place. From the Inconscience evolves Matter, from Matter Life, from Life Mind and from the Mind the Spirit. Sri Aurobindo says that "this is an evolution out of a material Inconscience into spiritual consciousness, an evolutionary self-building of Spirit on a base of Matter".[23] Therefore, the aim of evolution is to gradually manifest the hidden Spirit in Matter.

According to Sri Aurobindo, the process of evolution is governed by triple principle, namely, widening, heightening and integration. First, widening is an evolution of forms of matter proceeding from simple to more and more complex ones so as to admit the action of a complex and subtle form of Consciousness. Secondly, heightening is a progress of Consciousness from lower grade to higher grade. "All evolution is in essence a heightening of the force of consciousness in the manifest being so that it may be raised into the greater intensity of what is still unmanifest, from matter into life, from life into mind, from the mind into the spirit".[24] Thirdly, integration is taking up of all the lower grades and transforms them according to its own laws and principles. The principle of integration is this: "a taking up of what has already been evolved into each higher grade as it is reached and a transformation more or less complete so as to admit of a total changed working of the whole being and nature, an integration, must be also part of the process, if the evolution is to be effective".[25] This is a very important thing in the process of evolution in Sri Aurobindo's philosophy. To bring out the importance of the principle of integration, Prof. S.K. Maitra writes:

> There is no Eastern or Western philosopher who has stressed this very essential feature of evolution as Sri Aurobindo has done. The usual view of evolution, which locks upon it as a mere ascent from the lower grade to a higher grade, may be compared to the March of an army which advances without keeping its lines of communication with the base intact. And we may compare Sri Aurobindo's conception of evolution with the march of an army which advances with the whole force, keeping all its lines of communication perfectly intact.[26]

The aim of this evolutionary process is not only to deliver the terms involved in the Inconscience but eliminate the hold of the Inconscience on them by converting it into a kind of involved Superconscience. It aims at a radical change in the nature and working of the principles of the material world. To quote from Sri Aurobindo:

> The end of this triple process must be a radical change of the action of the Ignorance into an action of Knowledge, of our basis of inconscience into a basis of complete consciousness, — a completeness which exists at present only in what is to us the supraconscience.[27]

Further he writes:

> An evolution in the Inconscience is the beginning an evolution in the Ignorance is the middle, but the end is the liberation of the spirit into its true consciousness and an evolution in the Knowledge.[28]

Without the emergence of principles of Life and Mind, the liberation of Spirit into its true consciousness cannot be attained. They first transform the substance of matter into living substance and then into conscious substance. They succeed in changing it into a substance free from inertia, immobility and inconscience. But they do not succeed in transforming the nature and working of Matter altogether. They cannot make it completely alive and perfectly conscious. This clearly indicates that as long as the evolved term is in the grip of the Inconscience of Matter, a complete transformation of the physical foundation is out of the question. It also indicates that the total transformation of Matter depends on the emergence of a term which is absolutely free and unaffected by the conditions of the physical basis. Sri Aurobindo observes:

> If there is to be an entire transformation, it can only be by the full emergence of the law of the spirit; its power of supermind or gnosis must have entered into Matter and it must evolve in Matter. It must

> change the mental into the supramental being, make the inconscient in us conscious, spiritualize our material substance, erect its law of gnostic consciousness in our whole evolutionary being and nature. This must be the culminating emergence or, at least, that stage in the emergence which first decisively changes the nature of the evolution by transforming its action of Ignorance and its basis of Inconscience.[29]

In the previous stages of evolution change in the physical organization preceded the change of consciousness. That is to say, form-evolution preceded the evolution of consciousness. Since the force of consciousness already in formation was insufficient to effect a change in the body, change of consciousness was achieved by the change of the body. But in the case of man this method is likely to be reversed. It is through his consciousness, rather through a transformation of his consciousness, that a future evolution must be effected. Sri Aurobindo says that, this reversal corresponds to the inner reality of the forces of evolution. He says:

> In the inner reality of things a change of consciousness was always the major fact, the evolution has always had a spiritual significance and the physical change was only instrumental; but this relation was concealed by the first abnormal balance of the two factors, the body of the external Inconscience outweighing and obscuring in importance the spiritual element, the conscious being. But once the balance has been righted, it is no longer the change of body that must precede the change of consciousness; the consciousness itself by its mutation will necessitate and operate whatever mutation is needed for the body.[30]

If the method of evolution is reversed in man so as to give priority to the consciousness over the physical form, man becomes free enough to participate and accelerate the process of evolution in Nature. Man is no longer a witness to the workings of Nature and a passive recipient of the benefits of her workings. Therefore, in the future evolution man has a crucial role to play serving as a conscious and willing instrument at the hands of Nature.

The Triple Transformation

To attain a radical and integral transformation of the whole personality of man, which is the aim of the evolution Sri Aurobindo says the consciousness in man has to undergo the triple transformation, namely, the psychic, the spiritual and the supramental transformation. He writes:

> There must first be the psychic change, the conversion of our whole present nature into a soul-instrumentation; on that or along with that there must be the spiritual change, the descent of a higher Light, Knowledge, Power, Force, Bliss, Purity into the whole being, even into the lowest recesses of the life and body, even into the darkness of our subconscience; last, there must supervene the supramental transmutation, — there must take place as the crowning movement the ascent into the supermind and the transforming descent of the supramental Consciousness into our entire being and nature.[31]

The Psychic Transformation

The soul or psychic being is the highest representative of the Self in Man. It is "the permanent being in us, puts forth and uses mind, life and body as its instruments, undergoes the envelopment of their conditions, but it is other and greater than its members".[32] "It is an ever pure flame of the divinity in things and nothing that comes to it, nothing that enters into our experience can pollute its purity or extinguish the flame".[33] It always remains the same, though other parts in us are mutable and perishable. But presently the psychic entity is veiled in us by the conditions of its instruments. Therefore the first step needed towards an integral transformation consists in bringing the veiled psychic entity to our surface consciousness and making it an active principle of our life and existence. Psychicisation means the illumination of the surface mind, life and body by the light from within. When explaining the psychic transformation, Prof. Haridas Chaudhuri writes:

> Psychicisation means psychic change of the lower nature, bringing right vision into the mind, right impulse and feeling into the vital, right movement and habit into the physical-all turned towards the Divine, all based on love, devotion and adoration — and finally, the true vision and sense of the dynamic Divine (the Mother) everywhere in the world as well as in the heart. When the psychic comes to the front and assumes the reins of administration, progress in Integral Yoga is enormously accelerated and there is a sure and quick movement towards the dynamic realization of the Truth. It is this Psychicisation which can effectuate a true integration or harmonisation of our being, because the psychic entity is the central principle of integration within us.[34]

The Spiritual Transformation

If the psychic transformation is the first step of the

spiritual and supramental transformation, the second step is the transformation by the spiritual consciousness. In the words of Prof. Haridas Chaudhuri, "While Psychicisation means the joining of the depths of being to the surface, spiritualization means the uniting of the manifested existence with what is above it".[35] In the spiritual transformation, the ordinary consciousness of the mind grows into the higher grades of consciousness and existence that lies between mind and the Supermind. According to Sri Aurobindo, there are four grades of consciousness between mind and the Supermind. They are: Higher Mind, Illumined Mind, Intuition and Overmind respectively. The Overmind represents the highest limit of the Mental principle. It is somewhat similar to the supramental consciousness, but basically different in its function and organization. It is essentially a consciousness of cosmic unity, where individual mind is united with Cosmic Mind, individual self with Cosmic self. The unification issues out of the knowledge of the truth of terms united. All apparent contradictions are reconciled in the overmental consciousness. As regards global nature of the overmental consciousness, Sri Aurobindo writes:

> Overmind Consciousness is global in its cognition and can hold any number of seemingly fundamental differences together in a reconciling vision.[36]

The emergence of the overmental consciousness in man is marked by a universal consciousness and force and a manifold delight of being. The mental, vital and physical parts come under the influence of the overmind, feel a greater freedom in their movements.

But, the descent of the overmind into the human

organism will not effect an integral transformation. The transformation effected by overmental consciousness on the outer nature is more powerful and fundamental. But when it acts on it, its power is mutilated, its effect becomes partial and its movement fails to be fully effective, because the outer nature is still rooted in the ignorance and inconscience. Describing the effect of the overmental consciousness on the outer nature, Sri Aurobindo says:

> It would be as if a sun and its system were to shine out in an original darkness of Space and illumine everything as far as its rays could reach so that all that dwelt in the light would feel as if no darkness were there at all in their experience of existence. But outside that sphere or expanse of experience the original darkness would still be there and, since all things are possible in an overmind structure, could reinvade the island of light created within its empire.[37]

Therefore, the descent of the overmind does not change the basis of terrestrial nature and it is possible only by the supramental transformation.

The Supramental Transformation

If spiritual transformation, then, is not the final goal of integral evolution or integral yoga, the third and the final transformation is the supramental transformation. "As the psychic change has to call in the spiritual to complete it, so the first spiritual change has to call in the supramental transformation to complete it".[38] Therefore both the psychic and the spiritual transformations are inadequate. The most integral, inclusive and harmonious vision can be obtained by the Supermind and the Supermind alone.

The supramental change, is something radically different from what we conceive with our mental consciousness. Upto the stage of the Overmind, the evolution proceeds through ignorance. But with the descent of the Supermind the basis of ignorance is changed into that of knowledge. As the result of descent of supermind the overmental consciousness is transformed into the supramental. Supermind is the integral consciousness where there is no division, where God and man, Brahman and the world are one. It is the vast, as the Vedic *rishis* say. Supramental consciousness is all-containing, all-originating and all-consummating in its force and action. Its natural qualities are omnipresence, omniscience and omnipotence. When man ascends into the supramental consciousness he feels that he lives and acts in an entire transcedent freedom, a complete joy of the Spirit. To him all beings are his ownselves, all ways and powers of consciousness are the ways and powers of his own consciousness. He finds that, his own life and the world-life are like a perfect work of art. He is in the world and of the world, but also exceeds it in his consciousness as the transcendent self. The impact of the supramental consciousness in the working of his mind, life and body, is so radical and complete that all disharmonies and confusions cease to exist. To quote from Sri Aurobindo:

> The supramental transformation, the supramental evolution, must carry with it a lifting of mind, life and body out of themselves into a greater way of being in which yet their own ways and powers would be, not suppressed or abolished, but perfected and fulfilled by the self-exceeding".[39]

With the advent of supramental consciousness the whole outer being undergoes a final transformation. There will be a real participation by the individual in the working of the universal conscious-force. The valuable elements of outer nature are retained and uplifted. The distorting influence of the inconscience on the outer nature ceases to exist since it itself is transformed into supernature. This marks the beginning of Divine life upon earth.

REFERENCES

1. Dr. S. Radhakrishnan, *Indian Philosophy*, George Allen and Unwin, London, 1971, vol. II, p. 320.
2. Sri Aurobindo, *The Life Divine*, The Sri Aurobindo Library, INC, 1949, p. 13.
3. *L.D.*, p. 24.
4. *Ibid.*, p. 24.
5. *Ibid.*, p. 222.
6. *Ibid.*, p. 72.
7. *Ibid.*, p. 29.
8. *L.D.*, p. 106.
9. *Ibid.*, pp. 245-246.
10. *Ibid.*, p. 309.
11. *Ibid.*, p. 310.
12. *Ibid.*, p. 311.
13. *Ibid.*, p. 301.
14. *Ibid.*, p. 155.
15. *Ibid.*, p. 164.
16. *Ibid.*, p. 164.
17. *Ibid.*, p. 175.
18. *Ibid.*, p. 220.
19. *Ibid.*, p. 217.
20. *Ibid.*, p. 517.

21. *Ibid.*, p. 528.
22. *Ibid.*, p. 261.
23. *Ibid.*, p. 626.
24. *Ibid.*, p. 647.
25. *Ibid.*, p. 627.
26. S.K. Maitra, *An Introduction to the Philosophy of Sri Aurobindo*, Sri Aurobindo Ashram, Pondicherry, 1982, p. 44.
27. *L.D.*, p. 627.
28. *Ibid.*, p. 627.
29. *Ibid.*, p. 629.
30. *Ibid.*, p. 751.
31. *Ibid.*, p. 793.
32. *Ibid.*, p. 793.
33. *Ibid.*, P. 793.
34. Haridas Chaudhuri, *Sri Aurobindo: The Prophet of Life Divine*, Sri Aurobindo Ashram, Pondicherry, 1973, p. 75.
35. *Ibid.*, p. 78.
36. *L.D.*, p. 258.
37. *Ibid.*, p. 847.
38. *Ibid.*, p. 816.
39. *Ibid.*, p. 872.

Part - IV
Nature of Integral Yoga

CHAPTER 5

NATURE OF HUMAN PERSONALITY

Man and Mental Being

Since the aim of the Integral Yoga is to turn the whole human existence into Divine, it is necessary to understand its constitution, the difficulties that account for the present imperfections and possibilities of passing into a higher divine existence. From the ordinary point of view, man is regarded as essentially a mental being with its surface values. For the purpose of yogic development the idea that, man is a mental being is insufficient. Sri Aurobindo says that, "we have to travel beyond the physical nature and the superficial man and to discover the workings of the whole nature of the real man".[1] So what we need is to understand that the human personality is an organization of several psycho-physical factors with a spiritual foundation.

In his real nature man is spirit using the mind, life and body for self-manifestation in the world. The conditions of self-manifestation have created an apparent obscuration of the real nature of the spirit and its instruments, supermind, mind, life and body. An active principle of a spiritual perfection requires that we should pass beyond the surface obscurations and discover the real nature of man.

The Four Instruments

In order to manifest in the world, the spirit uses its four instruments: supermind, mind, life and body. Supermind is a self-conscious knowledge-will, sense, aesthesis and energy. Mind has all these powers though they are limited and partially luminous. Supermind is basically a principle of unity though it does not reject the principle of diversity. Mind is basically a principle of diversity though it can open itself to the higher principle of unity. Under normal conditions, mind is a source of ignorance. It always acts partially and by limitation. The mind also has a capacity to descend into a condition of complete inconscience, even as it can raise from ignorance to complete knowledge. By nature, supermind is incapable of real ignorance. Ignorance is not real in the sense it puts full knowledge behind the limitation of a particular working. While supermind allowing itself to the action of the lower instruments, it remains behind them as a secret support of their operations. When the outer veil of the lower instruments is removed, they find themselves organically related to supermind and acquire the qualities of the spirit as their natural properties.

Life is also an energy of the spirit. But it is subordinated to the action of the mind and body. It fulfills itself through mentality and physicality. It acts as a link between mind and body. Though, it has its own characteristic operation it never functions independent of mind and body. Generally, the energies of the spirit work in two terms of existence and consciousness. In the lower nature in which we presently live the energies of spirit work between the two terms of mind and matter. It supports the formulations of substance of matter and works as a material energy. In the same way, it supports the formulations of consciousness of mind and the functions of mental energy. Apart from these, it also supports the interaction of mind and body as a sensory and nervous energy.

Matter or body itself is a form of substance of spirit in which life and mind are involved. Life, mind and spirit are absorbed in their own externalizing action. By a process of evolution all that was involved in matter is bound to emerge and return to its natural form. It is possible for matter to become subtle and acquire formal density of life, of mind and of spirit.

Soul and Nature

According to another line of approach, the workings of spirit have two aspects, soul and nature. Soul is spirit cognizant of the workings of the nature. It supports them by its being. Nature is power of the spirit. It formulates form and name as being and develops action of consciousness and knowledge. Between soul and nature two kinds of relationship are possible. There may be a veil between the two, between spirit in supermind and spirit in mind, life and body. Where there is a veil between the two the instrumental powers are working in obscurity and imperfection. Where this veil has not fallen the instrumental powers are not what they are at present, but an enlightened part of supermind and spirit. When the soul is in the principle of mind using life and body it knows itself as a mental being working out its mental life and forces. When it lives in the principle of life, it knows itself as a vital being working out its impulsions and desires. When it dwells in the principle of matter, it knows itself as a consciousness of matter or a material being working out its own law of composition and decomposition. The soul in nature may lean towards the side of knowledge or ignorance. If it leans towards the former, it knows itself as a soul of mind, a soul of life and a soul of body. If it leans towards the latter it knows itself as an ego identified with mind, life and body, the triple formation of nature.

By the power of Yoga, man can become aware of the concealed parts of his personality and realize the existence of soul in his body, life and mind and finally, in supermind also. The path to integral perfection becomes clearly pronounced when man is able to discover the different levels of existence of spirit and identifies himself with it at all levels. Sri Aurobindo draws our attention to the importance of this upward effort, when he says,

> This present law of his being starts from the inconscience of the material universe, an involution of the soul in form and subjection to material nature; and, though in this matter, life and mind have developed their own energies, yet they are limited and bound up in the action of the lower material, which is to the ignorance of his practical surface consciousness his original principle. Mind in him, though he is an embodied mental being, has to bear the control of the body and the physical life and can only by some more or less considerable effort of energy and concentration consciously control life and body. It is only by increasing that control that he can move towards perfection,- and it is only by

developing soul-power that he can reach it. Nature-power in him has to become more and more completely a conscious act of soul, a conscious expression of all the will and knowledge of spirit. Prakriti has to reveal itself as Shakti of the Purusha.[2]

REFERENCES

1. *S.Y.*, p. 583.
2. *Ibid.*, pp. 589-590.

[illegible] dwell in any sphere of life [illegible] There [illegible] make no [illegible] the inner freedom [illegible] an outward dynamic working [illegible] forms and its sphere of external life.

[illegible] the personal [illegible] their work [illegible] realised the self [illegible] to work for [illegible] object and his own [illegible] for the spiritual [illegible] he does not take them [illegible] into account, for he serves [illegible] in the world. Therefore, he works [illegible] for the humanity. As Sri Aurobindo [illegible]

> [illegible] however, high [illegible] on the idea of our [illegible] its personal good [illegible] a release from suffering [illegible] of the trouble [illegible] the supreme aim of our existence. [illegible] desire of personal salvation [illegible] the complete rejection of [illegible] the Divine, it should be for the [illegible] for nothing else, because [illegible] call of our being, the deepest truth of the spirit.

Our [illegible] of men in whom the desire for personal salvation was less predominant than the compassion for the suffering humanity.

CHAPTER 6

THE RELEASE OF THE MENTAL BEING

The Three Mental Intuitions

Man is characteristically a mental being. Mentality is his highest present state in which he is nearest to the real Self. The way to perfection is not to involve in the outward or superficial existence. Nor is it to be identified with the soul of life or with the soul of body. He can reach the goal of perfection if he lifts himself above the physical, vital and mental levels. There are three mental intuitions on which he must place his exclusive emphasis: (a) The first one is the intuition of himself as someone observing the action of the mind. He finds himself as a witness *purusha* who watches nature and sees it as an action reflected upon the consciousness and enlightened by the consciousness. In itself, *purusha* is other than nature. The mental *purusha* finds that, it is no longer limited by the creation of the nature. It can give the nature's creations new directions and extensions. It is able to act in a mental world of more subtle and flexible creations. (b) The second one is the intuition of something larger and greater than the present action in which man lives. This allows him to stand upon the threshold of a subliminal self which opens to self-knowledge. (c) The last one is the greatest of all the three intuitions. It is the inner awareness of something which is far superior to mind as mind is far superior to physical life and body. This permits him to be aware of the supramental and spiritual being. When these three intuitions are well established in man, it is a clear indication that, he has gone beyond the surface confusions of the normal mentality and emerged into the perfection of the mental being, *Manomaya purusha*.

Two Possibilities

Now there are two possibilities: (a) When man possesses his mental being he can move in a direction away from existence and nature. It is a detachment and a withdrawal from life, mind and body. He lives more and more as the witness person and looks upon the action of nature without any interest. When this attitude takes an extreme form, it leads to a total withdrawal from the nature into pure conscious existence. This is the kind of liberation which the Sankhya has placed before us. (b) If the aim is to be not only free from nature but perfected in mastery, we have to find out the knots of bondage and loosing points of liberation in nature. We have to lay our finger on the key of perfection of nature. Initially, we find that nature is an automatic machinery. But, on a closer view that this is not completely true. The nature does not proceed of its own impulsion by the power of its mechanism. In actual fact, the action of nature continues because of the sanction of the *purusha*. We discover that without *purusha* nature cannot continue to act and when *purusha* withdraws its sanction, the habitual action of nature ceases. We realize that we are not only the upholding *purusha* but in some sense the master of nature. An absolute mastery over nature becomes possible only gradually. Though, we feel that whatever the nature is doing we have sanctioned it, a total rule over nature is not the immediate outcome. We are now in a position to choose between certain well-defined possibilities of nature. To this extent there is a certain mastery over nature. But still there is a power of resistance in nature because of its past impetus and also because of the sum of fixed conditions created by the past workings. This creates a duality of dependence. Nature depends on the consent of *purusha* and *purusha* depends on the law and limits of nature.

Absolute Control over Nature

The problem now is how to get absolute control over nature. We are aware that such a control is possible. If we can find it we will become not only the passive sanctioning witness and upholding soul of nature's will, but the free powerful user and determiner of nature's movements. But evidently this control seems to belong to another level than the mentality. It is a supramental control, a power of the spirit greater than mental being. To obtain control and lordship we must enter into identity with that supramental spirit. There are three possibilities now: (a) We can identify with the spirit by a sort of reflection and receive it in our mental consciousness. If we do so we become only a mould or an instrument. We do not possess or participate in the power of the spirit. (b) We can arrive at an identity by our absorption of our mentality in the spiritual being. But this leads to a trance of identity and all conscious actions ceases. (c) A third possibility is to raise to the supramental level where there is not only a passive but an active identity with the controlling spirit. We now become active master of nature whose will and movement are completely in our control. As the Taittiriya Upanishad says, we have to draw our mental being into the greater knowledge Being *vijnanamaya purusha* and then into the Bliss-self of the spirit, *anandamya purusha*. This is the utmost way of perfection.

Usually, the mixed and confused action of nature is a great obstacle to raise from the mental being into the supramental spirit. Therefore, the mixed and confused action has to be mended. This can be done by purification which is an essential means to self-perfection. Purification is to be followed by liberation, perfection and delight of being. In fact, they are the four constituent elements of Integral Yoga: *shuddhi, mukti, siddhi* and *bhukti*.

Of these four, the fourth namely *bhukti* is a natural consequence that follows on the establishment of the first three. Perhaps this is the reason why Sri Aurobindo concentrates only on the first three components of Integral Yoga and leaves out the fourth.[1]

Shuddhi is purification of our nature, a process by which the dependents of the higher on the lower nature is eliminated; *mukti* is liberation of the soul from its false identification with the outer nature as well as liberation of our nature from the limitations of the three *gunas; siddhi* is the replacement of the human energy by the Divine *shakti* in our system; *bhukti* is spiritual possession and enjoyment through participation in the cosmic play of the Divine.

A second difficulty which we have to deal with in order to arrive at complete perfection is the stress on individuality. We are identified with the physical, vital and mental ego. Unless, this identification with the triple ego is dissolved, it is not possible to abandon our separative individuality. In actual fact, it is not enough to give up identification with the ego. But we must arrive in the soul at a true universalized individuality in place of the separative individual formation. It is essential to universalize ourselves and become one with the Universe. This unification can come only through the soul by making the soul of mind one with the universal mind, the soul of life one with the Universal Life-Soul, the soul of body one with the Universal soul of physical nature. The unification with the Universal has several degrees depending upon the power, intensity, depth and permanence with which the relationship is maintained.

REFERENCE

1. See the bibliographical note to the sixth edition (1976) of *the Synthesis of Yoga*. The Synthesis of Yoga as a whole was never completed. Not only was the "Yoga of Self-Perfection" left unfinished, but a proposed additional section was not begun".

   Note that part three (Integral Yoga) of the present work is based on part IV of the Synthesis of Yoga, The Yoga of Self-Perfection.

CHAPTER 7

PURIFICATION (*SHUDDHI*)

Nature of Purity

A purification of the working of the instruments of the spirit is the first necessity in Integral Yoga. The spirit is forever pure. It is never affected by the faults of its instrumentation or the defects of mind and heart and body. Therefore, the spirit stands in no need of purification. Since mind, heart and soul of vital desire, the life with the body are the seats of impurity, they have to be purified. Unless their purification is achieved the working of the spirit through these instruments cannot be a perfect working or free from the limitations imposed by the lower nature. Generally, purity of the being is understood as freedom from sin. It is gained by an inhibition of whatever action which is considered to be wrong. This leads to a complete stilling of the vibrant mind and the soul of desire. Upon this, a Supreme peace enters and the spirit appears in all the eternal purity of its immaculate essence. Beyond this there is nothing to be gained. But for Integral Yoga, purification is a more difficult problem. It is not sufficient if the instruments are free from the present imperfect workings. For Integral Yoga, mind, heart, life and body are to do the works of the Divine, all the works which they do now and yet more. They have to do the works divinely. The object is therefore not a negative or passive, but a positive, affirmative and active purity. Sri Aurobindo describes the nature of works done divinely when he speaks about the active integral perfection and its effect on the seeker.

> His works will therefore, be the works of an eternal Knowledge, an eternal Truth, an eternal Might, an eternal Love, an eternal Ananda; but the truth, knowledge, force, love, delight will be the whole essential spirit of whatever work he will do and will not depend on its form; they will determine his action from the spirit within and the action will not determine the spirit or subject it to a fixed standard or rigid mould of working. He will have no dominant mere habit of character, but only a spiritual being and will with at the most a free and flexible temperamental mould for the action. His life will be a direct stream from the eternal fountains, not a form cut to some temporary human pattern. His perfection will not be a sattwic purity, but a thing uplifted beyond the gunas of Nature, a perfection of spiritual knowledge, spiritual power, spiritual delight, unity and harmony of unity; the outward perfection of his works will be freely shaped as the self-expression of this inner spiritual transcendence and universality.[1]

It is evident now that purification in Integral Yoga is radical and far more comprehensive than any process normally used for purifying the instruments of the spirit.

Two Forms of Impurity

An integral purification of the instruments demands that the defects of impurity have to be struck at their roots after a deeper diagnosis. There are two forms of impurity which are at the root of the whole confusion: (1) One is the defect born of the nature of our past evolution. It has been a nature of separative ignorance. The proper action of each part of instrumental being is given a radically wrong and ignorant form by this defect. (2) In the successive process of evolution life emerges in and depends on body. Then, mind emerges in and depends on life in the body. Finally, supermind emerges in and lends itself to mind. In other words, the second defect is caused by the dependence of the higher on the lower parts. It is an immixture of functions. Impure working of the lower instruments gets into the characteristic action of the higher function.

To take an illustration the proper function of the life is enjoyment and possession. Both these functions are perfectly legitimate. The world itself is created by the spirit for enjoyment and possession of the many by the one and of the one by many. But the separative ignorance gives to life the wrong form of desire and craving. This vitiates the whole enjoyment and possession. Want, suffering and opposites born of this separative ignorance are imposed on life. When mind evolves from life, it is entangled in the movements of life. The desire and craving of life get into the action of the mental will and knowledge. As a result, the rational will and discerning force of intelligence are turned into a will of craving and force of desire. The disinterested impartiality of a pure judgement and a rectitude of reason are no longer in existence. This is a case of immixture. These two defects are not restricted to these two instances. They belong to each instrument and to each combination of functions. If we can set right these fundamental defects of our instrumental nature, it can enter into a state of purity and enjoy the clarity of the pure will, a pure heart, a pure vitality and a pure body. This is however, a preliminary human perfection which can become the basis of Divine perfection.

Purification of the Buddhi

An analysis of the components of the instrumental being will be helpful to understand the higher form of divine perfection. A body supported by physical life force is the first instrument. *Prana* and physicality make the gross body *sthula sharira*. The second is the inner instrument, *antahkarana*. It is divided into four powers — *citta, manas, buddhi, ahankara*. The inner instrument constitutes the subtle body, *sukshma sharira*. Finally, there is a secret supermind beyond the conscious mentality. It is the in most instrument, and the proper means and the native seat of divine perfection.

We have said that, the initial human perfection comes when the two defects of the instruments are struck at their roots. Now the question is at what point purification begins. Even if one of the instruments is subject to purification, its complete purification is not possible because its purification depends upon the complete purification of all the others. The entanglement between the instruments is a great source of difficulty and perplexity. Therefore, we have to look for one important instrument which, when sufficiently purified can be used as a means for the purification of the others. Since, we are the spirit enveloped in the mind and a soul evolved here as a mental being in a living physical body, Sri Aurobindo points out that we must look for this effective instrument in the mind. Specifically, it is the *buddhi* in the mind which can serve as the most important instrument. Purification therefore, must begin with the *buddhi*, the intelligence and the will of the intelligence.

Before purification of the *buddhi* begins, a preliminary form of purification is necessary regarding the psychic *prana* which interferes in all higher operations and deforms them. The *psychic prana* itself is in the grip of the body. It has created the separation of the individual life from the life of the Universe. It has stamped on it the character of want, limitation, hunger, thirst, craving, groping after enjoyment and need of possession. Apart from this the psychic *prana* leans on the physical life and limit itself by the nervous force of the physical being. It brings in these limits into the operations of the mind. Our mind instead of being a clear instrument of conscious spirit becomes a mixed construction, a predominantly physical mentality subject to the obstructions of life in the body. The *psychic prana* is in the grip of desire, and if desire is completely removed all the deformations of the *psychic prana* are also eliminated. Its freedom from desire facilitate the purification of the inner instrument, *antahkarana*. This becomes the first step in purification.

From one point of view, the *buddhi* is the instrument of the soul by which some kind of possession of the soul as well as the surroundings become possible through the *buddhi*. It is impossible to get complete understanding or possession or mastery. This is so far the simple reason that the *buddhi* is only an intermediary instrument. The seat of complete understanding, possession of the mastery is elsewhere beyond the *buddhi*. But by itself it can give us a knowledge that there is a power within us greater than the animal life, a truth greater than the first truth perceived by the sense mind. It can also labour towards a greater and more successful power of action and control. To arrive at a complete self-fulfillment and integral perfection the *buddhi* as we have described above cannot help us fully. It will be a suitable instrument only when it is purified of all that makes its subject to the sense-mind and of all inherent limitations. In other words, its inferior mental intelligence and will must be converted into the greater action of spiritual will and knowledge.

The process of purifying the *buddhi* of its subjection to the sense-mind involves a greater and greater detachment from the control of the lower suggestions. The method Sri Aurobindo suggests is this.

> When we perform a sort of practical analysis of the thinking mind, cut away this element and hold back the higher reason free, observing and silent, we find that this current understanding begins to run about in a futile circle, repeating all its formed opinions and responses to the impressions of things, but incapable of any strong adaptation and initiation. As it feels more and more the refusal of sanction from the higher reason, it begins to fail to lose confidence in itself and its forms and habits, to distrust the intellectual action and to fall into weakness and silence. The stilling of this current, running, circling, repeating thought-mind is the principal part of that silencing of the thought which is one of the most effective disciplines of Yoga.[2]

The *buddhi,* as a result of this discipline, is now completely detached from the sense-mind and established in an entire self-government, equality and calm, *sama, samata* and *shanti.*

There is one more step to be covered in the process of purification. That is to say, the *buddhi* must be freed from its own inherent limitations. They are of two kinds. (1) Its realizations are only mental realizations. The supramental truth cannot be reached by mental realizations. (2) It is incapable of making an effective unification of the truths it seizes. It acts in a helpless limitation of ignorance, though it may hold a truth far greater than its action. The other alternative is to select some aspect of the Supreme spirit and cast itself into a luminous sleep. Upon this the soul passes away into some ineffable height of spiritual being.

If the soul from the mental being is lifted into the spiritual gnosis, it helps us to overcome the inherent limitations of the *buddhi*. The spiritual gnosis can be turned on the whole nature to divinise the human being.

REFERENCES

1. *S.Y.*, pp. 602-603.
2. *Ibid.*, pp. 625-626.

CHAPTER 8

LIBERATION (*MUKTI*)

Integral Freedom

With the purification of the mental being and *psychic prana* the first and preliminary condition for integral perfection has been fulfilled. Purification is a process of throwing away of limiting and obscuring imperfections and confusion. Purification of the mental being effects the freedom from desire. From purification of the *buddhi* leads to the freedom from the sense-mind. All these are a preliminary freedom preparing the ground for the freedom of the soul, *mukti*.

Normally, liberation is considered to be a rejection of all nature or an extinction of the natural existence into some ineffable state of spirit. This cannot be the aim of Integral Yoga. From the point of view of the Integral Yoga, liberation refers to the inner change which is indispensable to spiritual freedom which implies two things: (1) a rejection of the chief bonds and master knots of the lower soul nature; and (2) an opening into the higher spiritual existence. The Gita very clearly says that, the knots to be cut are four in number, desire, ego, the dualities and three *gunas* of Nature. To be free in the negative sense is to be desireless, egoless, equal in mind and soul and spirit and beyond the three *gunas*. In the positive sense of freedom, one must be universal in soul united in spirit with God and possessed of the highest divine nature, *madbhava*. Therefore, the full sense of liberation includes the liberation of the nature as well as the soul.

Spiritual Desirelessness

Already we refer to the freedom from desire as part of purification. But desire has a double knot, a lower knot in the *prana* and a very subtle knot in the soul itself. Desire is a craving of the life force. The ordinary man cannot function without it. If the desire is seen from above, it is nothing but a will of the spirit. It is the will of the spirit who creates the universal movement. It is the will of the universal spirit who supports the universal movement. And finally, it is the will of the free individual spirit who is the soul centre of the multiplicities. This will in its natural form is an effortless, spontaneous, self possessing blissful will. Once the individual soul moves away from the universal and transcendence and moves towards ego the nature will of the spirit changes. It becomes an effort and a straining with afflicting recoils and pain of labour. As long as this deviation in will is not removed, desire in a subtle form continue to exist. Even when the instruments are subjected to complete purification, the existence of this subtle desire can bring back all the desires already removed. In order to be completely free from desire not only the mental and *psychic* but the spiritual desire must be renounced.

Freedom from Ego-Sense

Ignorance and bondage have the support in the ego. No real freedom is possible so long as one has not conquered the ego-sense. The seat of ego is in the *buddhi*. It is responsible for taking the individualization of mind, life and body for a truth of separative existence. The ego is therefore turned away from the greater reconciling truth of the oneness of all existence. It is the ego idea which supports the falsehood of a separative existence. An effective remedy to get rid of this idea is to dwell on the opposite idea of unity. Till the ego is removed from the *buddhi* it takes all subtle forms in order to persist in us. We may think we are free from it but we are really acting as its instruments. A total extinction of the ego is possible only when there is oneness with the transcendental Divine and with Universal Being. When we live in the spirit, we enjoy in the spirit, our oneness with the universal existence, with the timeless Divine and with all other beings. But the moment the soul moves towards the mental limitation, there is a certain sense of spiritual separativeness. This may at any moment lapse into the ego-sense, ignorance and oblivion of oneness. The way to achieve integral liberation from ego is surrender of our whole being to the Divine. Sri Aurobindo writes:

> The way proposed for the Integral Yoga is a lifting up and surrender of the whole being to him, by which not only do we become one with him in our spiritual existence, but dwell too in him and he in us, so that the whole nature is full of his presence and changed into the Divine nature; we become one spirit and consciousness and life and substance with the Divine and at the same time we live and move in and have a various joy of that oneness. This integral liberation from the ego into the divine spirit and nature

can only be relatively complete on our present level, but it begins to become absolute as we open to and mount into the gnosis. This is the liberated perfection.[1]

Liberation from the ego and liberation from the will, that is, the nature of the desire are not two different methods, but two aspects of a single process.

Two Kinds of Freedom from Nature

From the side of the spirit the consent to accept the ego and the desire is the basis of its lapse into the lower movements and the subsequent loss of its Divine nature. A rejection of these things brings about the "liberation of the spirit". From the side of the nature there are two contributions which it imposes on the soul's experience. They are the *gunas* and the dualities. The *gunas* are the essential qualitative modes which constitute the whole basis of the inferior action of nature. The effects of these modes on the soul is a strife of opposites and a mixture of constant pairs of contraries. It is true that a complete liberation from the ego and the desire produces a superiority to the *gunas* and a cessation of the dual action. From the side of the nature there are two kinds of freedom: (1) a liberation from nature in a quiescent bliss of the spirit; and (2) a liberation of the nature into a divine quality and a spiritual power.

The Gunas

There are three modes of nature *sattva, rajas* and *tamas. Tamas* is the principle and power of inertia, *rajas* is the principle of kinesis, passion, endeavour, struggle and initiation, *sattva* is the principle of assimilation, equilibrium and harmony. The character of all action and experience is determined by these three qualities. The soul in nature is controlled by these qualities. It can be free only by raising above the qualities and rejecting them altogether. It can also become free by gaining a superiority to the *gunas* and a transformation of their working.

The action of the principle of *tamas* is of two kinds, inertia of force and inertia of knowledge. It is a source of sluggish in action and immobility, mechanical unconscious action which does not possess the idea of its own energy. *Tamas* is predominant in the material nature and in our physical being. *Rajas* is the source of strongest kinetic motor power and desire. Its strongest hold is on the vital nature. *Sattva* is a source of intelligence, reason, rational will and all efforts of assimilation. Its strongest hold is in the mind. A withdrawal from these three *gunas* produces a quietude and stillness in order to merge in the spirit. This quietestic release is not sufficient for the freedom of the integral perfection. What is needed is a liberation of the soul in nature perfect and self-existent whether in action or inaction.

Liberation from the Gunas

Now a question arises, Is it possible to speak of liberation of the soul in nature? The ordinary answer is that it is not possible, because all action is of the lower *gunas*. There are only two possibilities. Nature can be immobile or active. When it becomes immobile, the soul remains in its quietitude. When it is active the soul is subject to the strife and the imperfections of the *gunas*. Therefore, it is said that, liberation of the soul in nature is impossible. Sri Aurobindo says that, if we stand above the *gunas* and compel them to change into their higher equivalence, then liberation of soul in nature is possible. In fact, the three *gunas* are the three derivations of the original powers of the Divine. If they are compelled to change, they change into corresponding powers of the Divine. Sri Aurobindo writes:

> Tamas in the spiritual being becomes a divine calm, which is not an inertia and incapacity of action, but a perfect power, *shakti,* holding in itself all its capacity and capable of controlling and subjecting to the law of calm even the most stupendous and enormous activity: Rajas becomes a self-effecting initiating sheer Will of the spirit, which is not desire, endeavour, striving passion, but the same perfect power of being, *shakti,* capable of an infinite, imperturbable and blissful action. Sattva becomes not the modified mental light, *prakasha,* but the self-existent light of the divine, being, *jyotih,* which is the soul of the perfect power of being and illumines in their unity the divine quietude and the divine will of action.[2]

As a result of this transformation the soul in nature can freely act without the limitations of the *gunas.*

Liberation from the Dualities

The knot of duality is in ignorance which is unable to perceive the spiritual truth of things. The ignorance deals with the forces of life not with a mastery of their truths but with a shifting balance of pleasure and pain, joy and sorrow, liking and disliking. Ordinarily the approach is to get rid of the dualities by a total withdrawal from nature. It is sooner or latter followed by a departure into the silent self. But for the Integral Yoga this is not sufficient. When the *gunas* are compelled to change into their divine counterparts, the dualities also cease to exist. The liberation of the nature becomes one with the liberation of the spirit.

REFERENCES

1. *S.Y.*, p. 633.
2. *Ibid.*, p. 643.

Chapter 9

Perfection (*Siddhi*)

Equality

Purification and freedom are the two important prerequisites of perfection. Perfection in Integral Yoga means a divine spirit and a divine nature which make divine action possible in the world. It also means a divinizing of the whole human nature. Perfection is achieved in two stages. Initially, it refers to the establishment of equality in all parts of our being. The Gita identifies equality and yoga, *samatvam yoga ucyate*. Sri Aurobindo says that, "equality is a term of consciousness which brings into the whole of our being and nature the eternal tranquility of the Infinite".[1] With the establishment of equality, the human nature becomes eligible for the next stage of perfection. Now perfection consists in raising all the active parts of human nature to the highest condition of their power so that they are divinized into true instruments.

Normally, we are subject to the troubled and ignorant

outer consciousness which pulls us in different directions and we become a puppet moved by the motive forces of our nature. A perfect equality of spirit and nature helps us to get back from our outer nature and its motive forces into the inner kingdom of greatness and peace. The very nature of the divine is equality. He who wants to mould himself into a image of divine equality must become one with the Divine. Sri Aurobindo emphasizes the need to be one with the Divine in order to realize perfect equality. He says:

> The Divine is equal to all, an impartial sustainer of his universe, who views all with equal eyes, assents to the law of developing being which he has brought out of the depths of his existence, tolerates what has to be tolerated, depresses what has to be depressed, raises what has to be raised, creates, sustains and destroys with a perfect and equal understanding of all causes and results and working out of the spiritual and pragmatic meaning of all phenomena. God does not create in obedience to any troubled passion of desire or maintain and preserve through an attachment of partial preference or destroy in a fury of wrath, disgust or aversion. The Divine deals with great and small, just and unjust, ignorant and wise as the Self of all who, deeply intimate and one with the being, leads all according to their nature and need with a perfect understanding, power and justness of proportion. But through it all he moves things according to his large aim in the cycles and draws the soul upward in the evolution through its apparent progress and retrogressing towards the higher and ever higher development which is the sense of the cosmic urge. The self-perfecting individual who seeks to be one

in will with the Divine and make his nature an instrument of the divine purpose, must enlarge himself out of the egoistic and partial views and motives of the human ignorance and mould himself into an image of this supreme equality.[2]

The aim of perfection includes two things, self-mastery and a mastery of the surroundings. In the ancient language, they are called *svarat* and *samrat*, self-ruler and king. Man is bound by the lower nature, its grief and joy, pleasure and pain, desire and attachment, likes and dislikes, emotions and passions. To conquer them is the condition of the self-rule. Unless one is equal it is impossible to raise above the lower nature. One who is not self-ruler cannot become master of his surroundings. For the outer mastery knowledge, will and harmony are necessary. These come only as a result of inner conquest.

Emotional and Vital Being

A perfect equality must be established not only in the self but also in the nature. The first step in this direction is the conquest of our emotional and vital being. They are the sources of greatest trouble, of inequality and subjection to imperfection. The establishment of purification and freedom brings equality to these parts. In fact, equality is the very sign of liberation.

Desire is the impurity of *prana*. Elimination of desire from *prana* brings a content and satisfied life-soul. The real function of the *prana* is enjoyment and possession. Equality in the *prana* makes its enjoyment universal and massed concentration of spiritual bliss. It also makes its possession large and inward not dependent on the external conditions. Our heart is usually under the control of grief, wrath, hatred, fear, inequality of love, pain and sorrow.

By the equality of the heart we get away from these aberrations. We are open to the pure divine forces and impose their values on all that touch our emotional being. As there is no question of ascetic killing of life-impulse and its functions, here also there is no question of killing the emotional nature. Sri Aurobindo writes:

> All that presents itself here in our outward nature in perverse or imperfect forms has a significance and utility which come out when we get back to the greater truth of divine being. Love will be not destroyed, but perfected, enlarged to its widest capacity, deepened to its spiritual rapture, the love of God, the love of man, the love of all things as ourselves and as beings and powers of the Divine; a large, universal love, not at all incapable of various relation, will replace the claimant, egoistic, self-regarding love of little joys and griefs and insistent demands afflicted with all the chequered pattern of angers and jealousies and satisfactions, rushing to unity and movements of fatigue, divorce and separation on which we now place so high a value. Grief will cease to exist, but a universal, an equal love and sympathy will take its place, not a suffering sympathy, but a power which, itself delivered, is strong to sustain, to help, to liberate. To the free spirit wrath and hatred are impossible, but not the strong Rudra energy of the Divine which can battle without hatred and destroy without wrath, because all the time aware of the things it destroys as parts of itself, its own manifestations and unaltered therefore in its sympathy and understanding of those in whom are embodied these manifestations. All our emotional nature will undergo this high liberating transformation; but in order that it may do so, a perfect equality is the effective condition.[3]

Like vital and emotional parts, the will and the thinking mind have to possess equality if they are to be used for divine action. A perfect equality in the will does not respond to the lower impulses. On the contrary, it waits for a greater impulsion from the light above the mind. It will not judge in the light of the mind, but wait for a greater direction from the above. The more it allows itself to be governed by the forces beyond mind the more it becomes one with the divine nature. The equal thought mind will not be bound by the dualities of our limited nature. The significance of ignorance and error are completely changed. It sees a knowledge imprisoned in ignorance, a truth in error. This equality is the most difficult to achieve. Only when the supramental light falls fully on the thinking mind the perfect equality in it becomes possible.

Four Aspects of Perfection

We have said that the perfection is achieved in two successive stages. In the first stage, perfect equality is established in the self as well as in the nature. In the second stage, the instruments are raised to their highest power of spiritual and divine action. There are four aspects to this second stage in the process of achieving perfection — *shakti, virya, daivi prakriti* and *shraddha.*

The instruments refer to the thinking mind, the heart, the *prana* and the body, *shakti* is the full powers of the members of the instrumental nature. *Virya* is the perfected dynamics of the soul-nature. *Daivi prakriti* is the assumption of the instruments into the action of the Divine power. *Shraddha* is a perfect faith in all the members to call and support the assumption.

Shakti

Of the four instruments, we shall begin with the

body. It is not only the outer instrument of the physical action but a base for all inner actions. When the working of the mind or spirit is expressed through the body, the body imposes its natural limitations on the action of the higher parts. It has a subconscient part which preserves the past habits of the mind and the vital. Naturally, it prevents any radical transformation of human nature which implies a dissolution of the past habits. The seekers of perfection feel that the body is a great impediment. One common approach is to suppress completely or to a greater extent the influence of the body. But to the seeker of the Integral Yoga the body is as important as any other instruments. It should be put to right use and not neglected, suppressed or abolished. "It must be taught an entire passivity in the hands first of the higher instruments, but eventually in the hands of the spirit and its controlling and informing Shakti. It must be accustomed not to impose its own limits on the nobler members, but to shape its action and its response to their demands, to develop, one might say, a higher notation, a higher scale of responses".[4]

The *prana* is a force for the action of physical and vital energy. It also supports the mental and spiritual action. It is therefore, necessary to have a complete control over the *pranic* force. In the Vedic image, it is a steed and the conveyance of the embodied mind and will. Whether the mind can go on the course of its action without any obstruction or whether its will and activity are restricted depends on the condition of the *pranic* force. The *pranic* force is necessary even for the supramental action. In fact, it is transformed into a supramentalised power.

Psychic prana has its centre in the heart. The heart becomes perfect when gladness-clearness and purity in the psychic life-being are established. It must also be poised in a complete equality. It must be trained not to make demands or impose itself on heart, mind or spirit. It must accept with a strong passive and active equality whatever impulsion comes to it from the spirit through the channel of the still mind. The *psychic prana* has two natural functions, possession and enjoyment. When it is elevated these two natural functions are also given full recognition and scope for perfect expression. In fact, there is a fourfold perfection of *psychic prana*. They are fullness, clear purity and gladness, equality, and capacity for possession and enjoyment.

The intelligence and thinking mind must be freed from both the vital and the emotional subjection. It must be free from its own inherent limitations. It must become an unsullied mirror of the truth. Like the *psychic prana* it has a four-fold perfection. They are purity, clear radiance, rich and flexible varity and integral capacity.

Virya

It is not enough to raise the instruments of human nature to their highest condition of power and capacity though it is very necessary. What makes the power of these instruments effective and gives them their type and direction is the force of the temperament, character and soul-nature. Therefore, it is necessary to free this force, *virya,* from its limitations. Without a perfected force of soul-nature the divine soul in us cannot act fully in the human instruments. When the soul-nature is liberated, it manifests as the universal force which is the force of the Supreme Master. To quote from Sri Aurobindo:

> The force at work in us must be the manifest divine Shakti, the supreme or the universal Force unveiled in the liberated individual being, *Para prakrtir jivabhuta,* who will be the doer of all the action

> and the power of this divine life, *karta*. The One behind this force will be the Ishwara, the Master of all being, with whom all our existence will be in our perfection a Yoga at once of oneness in being and of union in various relations of the soul and its nature with the Godhead who is seated within us and in whom too we live, move and have our being.[5]

The soul-nature or *svabhava* is a combination of the force of the soul and the mould of our nature. The original soul-force is modified by the particular mould of the nature which constitutes our temperament and character. The original force of the divine, when modified by the moulding influence of our nature, represents itself as a fourfold effective power, a power for knowledge, a power for strength, a power for mutuality and interchange, a power for works and service. Our ancient scripture refers to this fourfold expression of the soul-force in human nature, as *'Brahmana'*, *'Kshatriya'*, *'Vaishya'* and *'Shudra'*. Sri Aurobindo says:

> The ancient thought of India conscious of this fourfold type of active human personality and nature, built out of it the four types of the Brahmana, Kshatriya, Vaishya and Sudra, each with its spiritual turn, ethical ideal, suitable upbringing, fixed function in society and place in the evolutionary scale of the spirit... The psychological fact is that there are these four active powers and tendencies of the Spirit and its executive Shakti within us and the predominance of one or the other in the more well-formed part of our personality gives us our main tendencies, dominant qualities and capacities, effective turn in action and life. But they are more or less present in all men, here manifest there latent, here developed, there subdued and depressed or

subordinate, and in the perfect man will be raised up to a fullness and harmony which in the spiritual freedom will burst out into the free play of the infinite quality of the spirit in the inner and outer life and in the self-enjoying creative play of the Purusha with his and the world's Nature-Power.[6]

There are therefore, four types of human personality and all human beings fall into these four types. Development of personality not only means a perfection of a given psychological type but also a corresponding growth into other psychological types which are inherent in human nature. No type will be complete if it does not include something of the other types. The man of knowledge can serve truth with freedom and perfection only if he has intellectual and moral courage. Otherwise, he becomes a ritual priest. He cannot use his knowledge to the best advantage if he does not possess the skill to apply his knowledge for practical results. Otherwise, he lives only in the idea. He cannot also consecrate his knowledge fully if he does not possess the spirit of service to the humanity. The man of power must govern his force by knowledge. Otherwise, he becomes mere *asura*. He must also have the skill which will help him to use his strength, creatively and fruitfully. Otherwise, he becomes a storm that passes and devastates more than it constructs. He must also be obedient and use his strength as a service to God and the world. Otherwise, he becomes a selfish dominator. The man of productive mind and work must have an enquiring mind. Otherwise, he is without expansive growth. He must have courage and enterprise and the spirit of service. Otherwise, he cannot help the fruitfulness of the surrounding life by which he lives. The man of labour and service must possess knowledge and skill. Otherwise, he becomes a slave of society. Thus, it is necessary for each individual to develop a complete personality which is not restricted to one type but includes the qualities of all the four types. Explaining the significance of a complete development of the human personality in order to serve as a perspect channel for the divine force, Sri Aurobindo writes:

> Man is not cut out into an exclusive type of one of these dharmas, but all these powers are in him at work at first in an ill-formed confusion, but he gives shape to one or another in birth after birth, progresses from one to the other even in the same life and goes on towards the total development of his inner existence. Our life itself is at once an inquiry after truth and knowledge, a struggle and battle of our will with ourselves and surrounding forces, a constant production, adaptation, application of skill to the material of life and a sacrifice and service.[7]

Daivi Prakriti

Though, we raise to the higher levels of perfection by raising the instruments of our nature to the maximum power and capacity and enlarging the limits of our personality type, it is not enough to divinize the human instrument. To divinize it, the divine *shakti* must be allowed to replace our limited human energy. It is the ego sense in us which makes human energy limited and erects a wall between the infinite energy of the divine and the human instrument to which it is canalized. Though, the ego was necessary for the development of the lower life, it is an obstacle for higher life. Elimination of ego is an indispensable condition for higher life. The first step in overcoming the ego sense is to see that we are not the originators of action but that it is rather the divine power that acts in ourselves and in all others. This is the rule laid down by the Gita for those who follow the path of 'Karmayoga'. Though, this is helpful in overcoming the ego, it does not eliminate it. It only diminishes the control of the ego.

When we draw back from the workings of Nature in our lower normal being and raise the purified nature into a higher spiritual being, we are no longer a witness but become identified with the Divine as the master of his Nature, *prakriti*. This is an effective method in eliminating the ego. There is also another process by which the elimination of ego is achieved. In the first stage, we are aware of the Supreme power, receives it into our soul and uses it under the direction of the Divine. There is a sense of being subordinate doer. In the second stage, the individual doer disappears. It is this power which takes shape as thought in the mind. The individual has no sense of himself thinking, but of the divine power thinking in him. He feels that all his thought, will and act just happen in his system. In the third stage, there is an increasing manifestation of the divine in all our being and action. The sense of separate identity completely disappears. All our consciousness becomes the consciousness of the Lord; all our knowledge the knowledge of the Lord, all our thought, all our will and all our feeling are the thought, will and delight of the Lord. When this identity with the Divine *shakti* is established, we become a perfect vehicle for the divine energy to manifest without any obstructions or limitations.

Shraddha

The first three components of perfection do not have any significance in the absence of the fourth component namely faith, perfection of the human instruments and the soul-nature and the elimination of the ego become possible only when there is a proportionate growth of faith in us. Without faith it is difficult to take any step forward to a yet unrealized perfection. Sri Aurobindo says:

> The three parts of the perfection of our instrumental nature... the perfection of the intelligence, heart, vital consciousness and body, the perfection of the fundamental soul powers, the perfection of the surrender of our instruments and action to the divine Shakti, depend at every moment of their progression on a fourth power that is covertly and overtly, the pivot of all endeavour and action, faith, *shraddha*.[8]

Faith, in order to be perfect, must be an assent of our whole being to the truth seen by it. Basically, it is the soul's own will to become its idea of self and things. The belief of the intellect, the consent of the heart and the desire of the life-mind to possess and to realize are mere outward figures.

First of all the faith must be abiding in the essential truth and principles of Yoga. The skeptical doubt and the constant carping of the critical intellect are great obstacles to progress and enemies of faith. The seeker of the Integral Yoga must give up these two imperfections. The ideal of Integral Yoga may appear to be an impossibility to a normal intelligence, or it may be considered by many who have spiritual experience to be a kind of wild imagination. But the seeker of the Integral Yoga must refuse to give credit to these suggestions. What is demanded of him is an unflinching faith in the ideal of the Integral Yoga. It is not enough if the faith is in the fundamental principle or the ideas of the Yoga. It must also be a working faith in the power in us to achieve. Sri Aurobindo says, "a working faith must be a large assent to the suggestions and steps of the Divine power. It is a faith fixed on realities. In other words, the faith required of the seeker is a fuller and a stronger assent of the whole being to the presence and the guidance of the Divine power."

The Divine power expresses itself as 'Maheshwari', goddess of the supreme knowledge; as 'Mahakali', goddess of the supreme strength; as 'Mahalakshmi', goddess of the supreme love and delight; and as 'Mahasaraswati', the goddess of the divine skill and of the works of the spirit. A faith in the divine power is a faith rooted in all these four manifestations. Behind the divine power is the divine beings, *Ishwara*. Faith in the divine power must be extended to the divine being which is the ultimate support of the divine power.

REFERENCES

1. *S.Y.*, p. 647.
2. *Ibid.*, pp. 653-654.
3. *Ibid.*, p. 658.
4. *Ibid.*, p. 681.
5. *Ibid.*, p. 690.
6. *Ibid.*, p. 692.
7. *Ibid.*, pp. 698-699.
8. *Ibid.*, p. 718.

Part - V

Integral Yoga and the Concepts of Other Yogas

Chapter 10

Integral Yoga and the Yoga of Works

Works and Sacrifice

Generally, works are performed for the sake of our ego. As long as works are means to fulfill the demands of the ego, they strengthen the forces of the ego and continue to keep us in bondage. In order to become free from the ego, works have to be performed not with a view to serve the purposes of the ego but to dissolve the ego and its demands. It consists in doing works as a sacrifice to the Divine in us. In other words, works have to be performed not for the sake of the ego but for the sake of the Divine in the world. This is the significance of the declaration of the Gita. "By doing works otherwise than for sacrifice, this world of men is in bondage to works; for sacrifice practice works, O son of Kunti, becoming free from all attachment".[1]

In a general sense the law of sacrifice is already in operation. Even ordinary life conforms to this law. Though the attitude of the ego is that it alone is important and that it alone exists in the world, in practice it is compelled to function in the opposite direction. Often ego is compelled to function in such a way that it has to recognize, without a conscious admission, the supremacy of something other than itself. As Sri Aurobindo observes, "Indeed sacrifice is imposed and, where need be, compelled by the universal World-Force; it takes it even from those who do not consciously recognize the law-inevitably, because this is the intrinsic nature of things".[2] If the law of sacrifice is rooted in the very nature of things, doing works for the sake of ego is not absolutely true. But the fact remains that, our works are influenced by the considerations of the ego and the egoistic values. The seeming contradiction is accountable in the sense that, while the law of sacrifice operates unconsciously, the surface life is ignorant of the law and tries to achieve the aims of the ego as if the law of sacrifice is not indispensable. The law of sacrifice becomes really effective when it is consciously recognized and the conscious parts of our being give their consent. Now, the law becomes a means of freedom and joy. When the law takes hold of our conscious parts it expresses itself as a complete and unreserved self-giving. It awakens the consciousness of the one common self in the given and the object of the sacrifice.

The essence of sacrifice is not self-immolation or self-mortification; it is self-giving and self-fulfillment. The ultimate aim of the sacrifice is a transformation of our natural human parts into divine members. Therefore, our sacrifice is not giving without any return. It is rather an interchange between the embodied soul and the conscious nature in us and the eternal spirit. Though no return is demanded a marvelous return is inevitable. When our works are performed as works of sacrifice, it is ego that is surrendered; in place of the ego the infinite riches of the Divine power and presence establish themselves.

When works are offered as sacrifice, the works are not limited to a particular field of life. For the seeker of the Integral Yoga our whole life should be turned into a conscious sacrifice. All our actions must be brought under the law of sacrifice. Ordinary distinctions between the smallest and the greatest, the most ordinary and the most uncommon, the trifling and the noble, disappear. To reproduce the words of Sri Aurobindo on the nature of sacrifice as a conservated living.

> Our individualized nature must live in the single consciousness of an inner and outer movement dedicated to Something that is beyond us and greater than our ego. No matter what the gift and to whom it is presented by us, there must be a consciousness in the act that we are presenting it to the one divine Being in all beings. Our commonest or most grossly material actions must assume this sublimated character; when we eat, we should be conscious that we are giving our food to that Presence in us; it must be a sacred offering in a temple and the sense of a mere physical need or self-gratification must pass away from us. In any great labour, in any high discipline, in any difficult or noble enterprise, whether undertaken for ourselves, for others or for the race, it will no longer be possible to stop short at the idea of the race, of ourselves or of others. The thing we are doing must be consciously offered as a sacrifice of works, not to these but either through them or directly to the One Godhead; the Divine Inhabitant who was hidden by these figures must be no longer hidden but ever present to our soul, our mind, our sense. The workings and results of

> our acts must be put in the hands of that One in the feeling that that Presence is the Infinite and Most High by whom alone our labour and our aspiration are possible. For in his being all takes place; for him all labour and aspiration and taken from us by Nature and offered on his altar. Even in those things in which Nature is herself very plainly the worker and we only the witnesses of her working and its containers and supporters, there should be the same constant memory and insistent consciousness of a work and of its divine Master. Our very inspiration and respiration, our very heart-beats can and must be made conscious in us as the living rhythm of the universal sacrifice.[3]

The sacrifice of works thus performed compels us to renounce all the inner supports of egoism. It eliminates the seed of egoism out of our nature. All is done for the Divine and all is directed towards the Divine. All works and life become a daily dynamic worship and service of the Divine.

From the point of view of the Integral Yoga, the sacrifice of works produces two important results. It leads towards the highest devotion possible. The seeker possesses a growing sense of the Divine in all things and communes with the Divine in all his thought, will and action. He becomes an active and effective representation of the very spirit of self-devotion. An absorbing love for the Divine, a Universal love for all beings is the inevitable result of his consecrated life. In consequence, "the way of works turns by this road of sacrifice to meet the path of Devotion; it can be itself a devotion as complete, as absorbing, as integral as any the desire of the heart can ask for or the passion of the mind can imagine".[4] This is the first result of the sacrifice of works. The second result is that, the way of works gradually issues into the way of knowledge. The sacrifice of works, when performed in all inclusive form leads to a seeing, as concrete as physical sight, of the works of the Universal Divine in everywhere. Whatever the seeker sees and hears, touches and senses all is turned into an image of God and perceived as a dwelling place of the Godhead. The way of works thus, turns into a way of knowledge.

Works and the Annihilation of Ego

Surrender of all desire for the fruit of our works is an essential element in the sacrifice of works. The Gita says, "To action thou hast a right but never under any circumstances to its fruit".[5] Until, we work with attachment to the result our sacrifice is offered not to the Divine but to our ego. The fruit belongs entirely to the Lord of works. Our only concern with the fruit is to prepare the success by a true and careful action and to offer it to the Lord. It is not enough if we abandon attachment to the fruit; we must also abandon attachment to the work. At any moment we may be called upon to change one work for the another. Or we may even be called upon to give up all works if that was necessary to accomplish the Divine purpose. Unless, we are willing to take an attitude of complete detachment towards work, we would still be subject to the influence of the egoism. We do the act not for the sake of the Lord but for our satisfaction and pleasure in the work. Not only the fruits but the work also belongs to the Lord. Besides renouncing our attachment to the work and its fruits, we are asked to renounce attachment to the idea and sense of ourselves as the doer. The last step in the sacrifice of works eliminates the central egoism which is the most difficult and cannot be perfectly done if the first two steps have not been taken.

But the first step too cannot be completed unless the third comes in and eradicates the very origin of desire. The significance of the triple renunciation is well brought out by the Gita. When it says, "The Lord neither creates the works of the world, nor the idea of being the doer, nor the coupling of works to their fruits; all that is worked out by the Nature in the man".[6]

The ego-sense of the worker becomes extinct gradually. To begin with the seeker ceases to regard himself as the worker. He firmly realizes that he is only an instrument of the cosmic force. This realization liberates the mind but not the rest of our nature. Though the egoism of the worker disappears the egoism of instrument may take its place. If we cherish the instrumental ego, we pretend to ourselves that we are conscious instrument of the Divine. In reality, we make the Divine an instrument of our own desires. Therefore, there must be no egoism of any kind in the attitude of the instrument. Our nature must admit the cosmic force but not in its lower aspect of *rajasic* or *sattwik* movement. It must admit the universal power in the light of a greater liberating knowledge. Everyone is an instrument of the universal power, whether he knows it or not. Basically, there is no difference between one action and another, one kind of instrumentation and another. What matters is the cosmic force which chooses this rather than that as the instrumentation for working out its purpose. As Sri Aurobindo says, "If the potter shapes one pot more perfectly than another, the merit lies not in the vessel but the maker".[7] Once the instrumental ego disappears we become pure instruments consciously consenting to every turn of the divine force that moves us.

For the seeker of the Integral Yoga, there is another step to be taken. It is not enough to surrender our instrumental ego to the Divine power. Though we realize that the Divine force uses our mind, life and body which have become spiritualized parts, there is still an imperfection in them. Though the dynamic parts in us are liberated from the ego-sense, they are not perfect in the sense that, they are still subject to the influence of the lower nature. For the Yoga of works the aim must be not only liberation but perfection of the dynamic parts of the instrument. After the removal of the veil of the ego, the removal of the veil of nature from our mind, life and body becomes inevitable.

When we become the pure instrument and allow the Divine force to be in direct touch with our dynamic parts, we no longer serve ego or ego-force. It is the Divine which we serve. There is a perfect understanding now of the mechanism and its utilization for his world purposes by the master of works. Our action is spiritually illumined, and to this extent it has become a faithful expression of the Divine will. But this opens up another possibility. It is possible for our dynamic parts to be transformed and uplifted into the greater supernature of the Divine. If the seeker is able to rise beyond the spiritualized mind and act spontaneously in the living presence of the Divine power. His mind, life and body are transformed and uplifted into the Divine nature. The transformed instrument is no longer a means but an integral part of the Divine supernature. The sense of separate identity of form or independent movement completely disappears. To quote from Sri Aurobindo:

> There is no longer the sense of ourselves moving, thinking or feeling but of that moving, feeling and thinking in us. This force that we feel is the universal Force of the Divine, which, veiled or unveiled, acting directly or permitting the use of its

> powers by beings in the cosmos, is the one Energy that alone exists and alone makes universal or individual action possible. For this force is the Divine itself in the body of its power; all is that power of act, power of thought and knowledge, power of mastery and enjoyment, power of love. Conscious always and in everything, in ourselves and in others, of the Master of Works possessing, inhabiting, enjoying through this Force, that is himself becoming through it all existences and all happenings, we shall have arrived at the divine union through works and achieved by that fulfilment in works all that others have gained through absolute devotion or through pure knowledge.[8]

Though the seeker of the Integral Yoga has gone far beyond the limited aim of liberation and achieved perfection by transforming the instrumental part into a substance of the Divine Nature, his achievement is limited to a cosmic identity with the Divine. His next step is to enter into the identity of the transcendent Divine. This indeed the supreme achievement by which the union of the soul as well as nature with the Divine becomes complete. On one side there is an infinite self-existent Godhead in being who contains all things, but is at the same time an illimitable person. On the other side the same Godhead is the effectuating consciousness and power put forth as a force that contains and carries all within it and is capable of manifesting them in time and space. In fact, there is one supreme and infinite being represented to us in two different sides of itself, obverse and reverse, in relation to each other. In this duality of *Ishwara shakti* lies the entry into the deepest secret of the transcendental Divine.

Works and the Divine Work

It is generally believed that desire, works and bondage are inseparable and interdependent. Desire is the motive for works, works fulfill the desire for embodied existence; by fulfilling the desire for embodied existence works lead to the bondage of the soul to the body. If works are turned into works of sacrifice it removes desire as a motive force and as a result free the soul from its embodied existence. When the soul realizes its freedom, it lives in the eternal presence of the Divine and the object of the embodied existence in the world is realized. The soul is now released not only from desire and bondage but also from the necessity of works. If the liberated soul were to act, it would be a derogation from the highest state and a fall into the life of ignorance.

It is held that even after liberation works may continue in order to work out the consequences of the previous *karma* which set in motion the presence embodied existence. According to another view, the liberated soul has really no work to do and has only to use works in order to fulfill the supreme will and do whatever it dictates. It is content to work in field and the cadre of the family, clan, caste, nation, occupation determined by his birth and circumstance. It has only to continue working in its own sphere assigned to it by its birth and circumstance till the great hour arrives when it can disappear into the infinite existence.

The view that considers works as a means to liberate the soul and realize individual freedom from the cycle of physical rebirth, necessarily looks upon works as a meaningless momentum for a liberated soul. The object of spiritual liberation is considered to be exclusively personal and individualistic. In attaining liberation of the soul from its bondage to the body the individual has to work for it and realize the aim by its own personal effects. No real help from outside is possible, because nobody else can work out the effect of past life and achieve spiritual freedom on behalf of another.

There is a significant verse in the Gita which says that, works should be performed in order to hold together the peoples, *lokasangraham*.[9] It is interpreted that works have to be performed by the liberated not because he has any personal use for them but because he has to set an outward example for the ignorant mass to adhere to the customary works laid down by the social law.

From the point of view of Integral seeker, the view that works generate bondage and cease on the attainment of spiritual liberation is not acceptable. For him all existence in the world is work and has a dynamic effect on the whole by its mere presence. Even the inertia of the clod is no exception to this rule. The manner of action, the instruments of action, the spirit and knowledge of the worker may change but works never cease. Because no man really works; it is Nature which works through him for the self-expression of a power within. What is required is freedom from desire and the illusion of personal impulsion. He must learn to live in the presence and the being of the master of Nature at whose will works take shape and realize their goal. What ceases is the bondage of works and not the works themselves. He now acts as the Divine Existence, acts without any binding necessity or compelling ignorance.

It is wrong to believe that works are impossible without desire. Even in ordinary conditions, before one is free from bondage, a major part of the work is accomplished without any interference of desire. It is governed by the calm necessity and spontaneous law of nature. Apart from works done in the universe, man does his works on most of the occasions by a spontaneous impulse without either mental planning or desire. Very often his actions are contrary to his intension or desire. Therefore, desire is not necessarily the motive force of works. Sri Aurobindo observes:

> Desire is an additional lure to which Nature has given a great part in the life of animated beings in order to produce a certain kind of rajasic action necessary for her intermediate ends; but it is not her sole or even her chief engine. It has its great use while it endures; it helps us to rise out of inertia, it contradicts many tamasic forces which would otherwise inhibit action. But the seeker who has advanced far on the way of works has passed beyond this intermediate stage in which desire is a helpful engine. Its push is no longer indispensable for his action, but is rather a terrible hindrance and source of stumbling, inefficiency and failure. Others are obliged to obey a personal choice or motive, but he has to learn to act with an impersonal or a universal mind or as a part or an instrument of an infinite Person. A calm indifference, a joyful impartiality or a blissful response to a divine Force, whatever its dictate, is the condition of his doing any effective work or undertaking any worth-while action. Not desire, not attachment must drive him, but a Will that stirs in a divine peace, a Knowledge that moves from the transcendent Light, a glad Impulse that is a force from the supreme Ananda.[10]

It is also wrong for the integral seeker to accept the view that, after liberation one should not insist on any particular end or work for some great mundane object.

After liberation a man may dwell in any sphere of life and in any kind of action and fulfill the Divine will. There are two alternatives: (1) the inner liberation may make no apparent difference in his outward acts, and (2) the inner freedom may translate itself into an outward dynamic working which changes the forms and its sphere of external life.

The integral seeker does not desire personal salvation. He thinks that though everybody must work out his own salvation, he who has already realized the self can help others to a very great extent. In fact, to work for the salvation of the others is the main object and his own personal self-realization is just a qualification for the spiritual service. Even while he serves others he does not take their caste or community or nation into account, for he serves only the Divine will in the world. Therefore, he works for the Divine rather than for the humanity. As Sri Aurobindo observes:

> The desire of personal salvation, however, high its form, is an outcome of ego; it rests on the idea of our own individuality and its desire for its personal good or welfare, its longing for a release from suffering or its cry for the extinction of the trouble of becoming and makes that the supreme aim of our existence. To rise beyond the desire of personal salvation is necessary for the complete rejection of this basis of ego. If we seek the Divine, it should be for the sake of the Divine and for nothing else, because that is the Supreme call of our being, the deepest truth of the spirit.[11]

Our cultural history is not without examples of men in whom the desire for personal salvation was less predominant than the compassion for the suffering humanity.

The Buddha is an outstanding example. He refused to enter into *nirvana* until even a single being is not released from suffering and pain. This was also the message of the famous verse in the *Bhagavata Purana* where the devotee says that, he does not desire the highest spiritual state of wielding spiritual powers or the cessation of rebirth and wants to be born again and again so that he can relieve the living beings of their misery by undergoing the suffering on their behalf. Swami Vivekananda also spoke in a similar vein, when he spoke that he was willing to be born again and again and suffer all the miseries of the living beings in the world.

The *sadhaka* of Integral Yoga would never subscribe to the interpretation put on the verse in the Gita which says that works should be done in order to hold together the peoples of the world. If the liberated man is to act in order to maintain the goal of social law, it takes away the deep and true sense of the Gita. Though works are a means for self-development and self-fulfillment, it is ultimately a means for the fulfilment of the Divine intention in the world. It is in this context that the message of the Gita is to be interpreted. To quote Sri Aurobindo:

> But if we accept rather the view that the world is a divinely guided movement of Nature emerging in man towards God and that this is the work in which the Lord of the Gita declares that he is ever occupied although he himself has nothing ungained that he has yet to win, than a deep and true sense will appear for this great injunction. To participate in that divine work, to live for God in the world will be the rule of the Karmayogin; to live for God in the world and therefore so to act that the Divine may more and more manifest himself and the world go

forward by whatever way of its obscure pilgrimage and move nearer to the divine ideal.[12]

REFERENCES

1. *B.G.*, pp. 3-9.
2. *S.Y.*, p. 94.
3. *Ibid.*, pp. 98-99.
4. *Ibid.*, p. 100.
5. *B.G.*, pp. 2-47.
6. *Ibid.*, pp. 5-14.
7. *S.Y.*, p. 228.
8. *Ibid.*, pp. 231-232.
9. *B.G.*, pp. 3-21.
10. *S.Y.*, p. 244.
11. *Ibid.*, pp. 246-247.
12. *Ibid.*, p. 249.

Chapter 11

Integral Yoga and the Yoga of Knowledge

Knowledge and its Object

It is traditionally held by those who follow the path of knowledge that the Absolute is a pure transcendent state beyond cosmic existence. All cosmic existence is regarded as a state of ignorance. The individual perfection, which may be of a very high order when compared with the ordinary achievements of human life, but it is no better than a Supreme ignorance. Because the perfection is still within the boundaries of the cosmic existence. He who seeks the supreme object of knowledge can do so only by eliminating all that is individual, all that is cosmic.

The Absolute is attained by an extinction of ego and all activities, mental, vital and physical. Action is needed only to purify the seeker so that he becomes qualified for the knowledge of the Absolute. Only those activities connected with the rites of worship and ordained by the sacred books are permissible. All other actions do not serve the purpose. These actions can only prepare salvation and cannot produce it directly. Once the needed purity is acquired actions must completely cease. For those who persist in works cannot realize the Absolute. Even worship is a method necessary for the unripe ignorant soul. Worship presupposes the duality of one who offers love and devotion and another who receives it. Since the knowledge of the Absolute has no place for dualities, worship as a discipline cannot lead to a non-dual realization. Even thought activity has to disappear if the non-dual Brahman is to be realized.

From the point of view of the Integral Yoga, the principle of elimination advocated by the traditional path of knowledge has a wider significance. The traditional method arrives at the transcendent Absolute by a process of elimination. The body, the life, the senses, the heart and the thought are successively rejected in order to enter into the state of silent Brahman. For the integral seeker this is a narrow method because it sees the reality only as transcendental existence. In his view, the real is not only beyond but also in and as the world. Therefore, what is to be eliminated is the ignorance and the results of ignorance. To quote Sri Aurobindo, the integral seeker would say,

> Eliminate the falsity of the being which figures as the ego; then our true being can manifest in us. Eliminate the falsity of the life which figures as mere vital craving and the mechanical round of our corporeal existence; our true life in the power of the Godhead and the joy of the Infinite will appear. Eliminate the falsity of the senses with their subjection to material shows and to dual sensations; there is a greater sense in us that can open through these to the Divine in things and divinely reply to it.

> Eliminate the falsity of the heart with its turbid passions and desires and its dual emotions; a deeper heart in us can open with its divine love for all creatures and its infinite passion and yearning for the responses of the Infinite. Eliminate the falsity of the thought with its imperfect mental constructions, its arrogant assertions and denials, its limited and exclusive concentrations; a greater faculty of Knowledge is behind that can open to the true Truth of God and the soul and Nature and the universe.[1]

If elimination is the chief process, thought is the chief instrument by which the object of knowledge is attained. The thinking consciousness separates itself from the phenomenal personality. It rejects the heart, draws back from the life and the senses and separates itself from the body in order to arrive at its own exclusive fulfillment in that which is beyond thought and mind. For the integral seeker there is a truth which underlies the self-negating function of thought. In a sense, thought is nearest to its aspect of the All-Conscious which regards all activities but can stand back from them all. In its most characteristic form it is a disinterested witness more than a participant and labourer. Therefore, its natural tendency is in the direction of an immobile transcendent being. The thought therefore, presents itself as an indispensable aid to our realization of the supreme state of knowledge. It is true that, it is the inner most door of the temple, but from a higher point of view it is not the real leader of the journey. In reality, the leader is the will. As Sri Aurobindo says that, "this Will is not the wish of the heart or the demand or preference of the mind to which we often give the name. It is that inmost, dominant and often veiled conscious force of our being and of all being. Tapas, Shakti, Shraddha, that sovereignly determines our orientation and of which the intellect and the heart are more or less blind and automatic servants and instruments".[2] This will is profounder and intimately nearer to the all-originating spirit, and the highest way for knowledge consists in knowing that in ourselves and in the universe and follow it to its divine finalities. When the seeker enters into the supreme will as the object of knowledge, not only the thought but the heart, the will and the body are entitled to receive their own satisfaction.

As the traditional system says, the path of knowledge need not necessarily entail extinction of our world-existence. The transcendent absolute which is the object of knowledge supports both the soul and the universe though it is beyond them. Therefore, there is no need to believe that our world-existence will come to an end on attaining the Supreme reality. The release into this highest state of silence and quietude represents the essence of one's conscious being. There remains on that foundation the infinitely proceeding self-fulfillment of the divine, its dynamic divine manifestation in the individual and the universe. Therefore, the liberated soul, *jivanmukta,* must work for the self-fulfillment through the acceptance of life and activities. Actions not only prepare but directly open the doors to the supreme reality, and having opened it they continue to serve as the means of fulfilling the supreme will in the individual and the universe.

Knowledge and Concentration

In the path of knowledge concentration is used as an effective method to remove the thought from all distracting activities of the mind. There are three ways of practicing concentration: (1) By concentration on anything we are able to know that thing. Though concentration may be used to discover the secrets of things, it must be used only to discover the one reality behind all things in the world. (2) By concentration, all aims can be fulfilled. Though it can be used to fulfill the aims which the world offers to us, its right use consists in the fulfillment of the supreme aim in life which is worthy of knowledge. (3) By concentration, we can become whatever we want to. For example, we can become a mass of strength and courage or an unlimited force of love by the power of concentration. But the proper use of this power must be for becoming the pure and the absolute spirit in us. Concentration is therefore, used in the traditional system as a method to arrive at an exclusive result, the knowledge of the transcendent reality beyond the universe and the individual.

From the point of view of the Integral Yoga, the aim of concentration is more complex and less exclusive. Its aim is indeed the highest source but not the exclusion of all that come out of the ultimate source. It does not seek to reject the consciousness of the universe but to realize God in the universe as well as transcendent of it. Concentration as a yogic discipline is an application by the individual of the principle by which the Lord of the universe is engaged in his creative activity. As Sri Aurobindo says:

> All our concentration is merely an image of the divine Tapas by which the Self dwells gathered in itself, by which it manifests within itself, by which it maintains and possesses its manifestation, by which it draws back from all manifestation into its supreme oneness.[3]

Specifically speaking, concentration as a yogic discipline becomes "the means by which the individual soul identifies itself with and enters into any form, state or psychological self-manifestation (*bhava*) of the Self".[4]

For the seeker of the Integral Yoga, there are three steps in concentration. (1) To accustom the discursive mind to a settle pursuit of a single course of connected thought on a single subject. Though in ordinary life a concentration of this kind is quite common, it is difficult to practice it in reference to something inward. This inward concentration is absolutely necessary for the seeker of knowledge. For example, if the divine love happens to be the subject of concentration, it is on the essence of the ides of God as love that we should concentrate. Once the knowledge and experience of the divine love arises, the practice of concentration should continue until the knowledge and experience become the very law of the being.

The next step in concentration is to reach the very essence of the thing behind the idea, the essence of divine love behind the idea. This becomes possible when thought ceases and passes into an absorbed condition. But this is not enough for the seeker of the Integral Yoga. He has to call this essential experience to take possession of the lower being so that it becomes part and parcel of our ordinary wakening consciousness.

The third step in concentration may be a way of stilling the mind altogether without following either of the first two steps, one may stand back from the mental action without participating in it. One simply watches it until it falls into an increasing and an absolute quiet or one may reject the thought suggestions from the mind and opens to the inner peace which exists behind the agitations of the mind. When this inner peace comes out, it becomes the firm basis for the complete manifestation of the divine in us.

Knowledge and Renunciation

Renunciation is an important discipline in the path of knowledge. There is an established tradition that renunciation must be practiced as an end. Renunciation means a complete abandonment of life and our earthly existence. There are several reasons why renunciation was understood in this sense. There is a natural opposition between the imperfect nature of life in the world and the nature of spiritual living. In order to realize the purity of the inner spiritual life, the life in the world is totally given up. This is the first reason. The second reason is the idea of personal salvation was irresistible, because the natural tendency is to remain in bliss and peace away from labour and struggle. Once the soul gets the taste of the ecstasy of the divine embrace there is an unwillingness to descend from that level and accept work and service at the physical level. This is the third reason. Even if one is not bothered by the opposition between the inner life and the outer life it is a great practical difficulty to combine the life of works with the life of spiritual realization. This is the fourth reason. The fifth reason is that the mind becomes attached to the joy in the act and the state of renunciation. The sixth and the last reason is the selfish desire to be free from the cycle of birth and death and all its consequences.

From the point of view of the integral seeker, renunciation must be an inward realization. It must be a renunciation of attachment and desire in the senses and the heart, of self-will in the thought and action and of egoism in the consciousness. They are the three knots by which the soul is bound to the lower nature; attachment, self-will and egoism. Attachment must completely vanish. Attachment may be of several forms. One may be attached to wealth or poverty, joy or suffering, life or death, vice or virtue, friend, wife, children, country a chosen work and mission, heaven or earth. Attachment in any form is not permissible. At the same time it does not mean that the integral seeker is not allowed to love or take delight in the object of the world. His love must be universal and his delight must be rooted in the delight of God. Self-will is attachment to the preferences, habits, formations of thought and will. Even this attachment must go. There must be willingness to give up one illumination in favour of another, one truth in favour of the higher truth. Egoism may persist in different disguises. Altruism and indifference are the most common disguises. A person allows himself to be influenced by altruism or indifference because he thinks that he can make best his impression on the environment. He is evidently guided by the opinion of men. But all these are expressions of egoism. Hence they must be dissolved.

Renunciation cannot be an end in itself. Because it is an instrument by which the knots of ignorance are removed. Once the knots are removed the integral seeker aims at the fulfillment of the Divine in life and world. His aim is not to shun human living because it is different from spiritual living. He has to solve the problem and discover the method of harmonizing both. He seeks personal salvation only as a necessity for the human fulfillment. He who is in bonds cannot free others. Therefore, personal salvation is not the goal but an essential qualification for doing service to humanity. Any form of unwillingness to come down from divine ecstasy in order to serve others is a sign of selfishness. Therefore, the integral seeker does not hesitate to give up that unwillingness. If the life of works and the life of spiritual realization cannot be combined, it is due to lack of effort and courage in the right direction. The integral seeker believes that his very mission it to arrive at a harmony of these two apparently opposite forms of existence. He never considers that the joy of renunciation is the only joy to be attained. The joy of possession and enjoyment for the Divine in the world is equally necessary. He never considers that life upon earth is one of suffering and cannot become an occasion for fulfillment and service to God.

In fact, he thinks that man is given a body only to realize God and express it in embodied life. To quote Sri Aurobindo on the meaning of the concept of renunciation:

> It will be seen that the scope we give to the idea of renunciation is different from the meaning currently attached to it. Currently its meaning is self-denial, inhibition of pleasure, rejection of the objects of pleasure. Self-denial is a necessary discipline for the soul of man, because his heart is ignorantly attached; inhibition of pleasure is necessary because his sense is caught and clogged in the mud-honey of sensuous satisfactions; rejection of the objects of pleasure is imposed because the mind fixes on the object and will not leave it to go beyond it and within itself. If the mind of man were not thus ignorant, attached, bound even in its restless inconstancy, deluded by the forms of things, renunciation would not have been needed; the soul could have travelled on the path of delight, from the lesser to the greater, from joy to diviner joy. At present that is not practicable. It must give up from within everything to which it is attached in order that it may gain that which they are in their reality. The external renunciation is not the essential, but even that is necessary for a time, indispensable in many things and sometimes useful in all; we may even say that a complete external renunciation is a stage through

> which the soul must pass at some period of its progress, though always it should be without those self-willed violences and fierce self-torturings which are an offence to the Divine seated within us. But in the end this renunciation or self-denial is always an instrument and the period for its use passes. The rejection of the object ceases to be necessary when the object can no longer ensnare us because what the soul enjoys is no longer the object as an object but the Divine which it expresses; the inhibition of pleasure is no longer needed when the soul no longer seeks pleasure but possesses the delight of the Divine in all things equally without the need of a personal or physical possession of the thing itself; self-denial loses its field when the soul no longer claims anything, but obeys consciously the will of the one Self in all beings. It is then that we are freed from the Law and released into the liberty of the Spirit.[5]

Knowledge and the Release from the Ego

In spiritual life, as in mundane life, the fulfillment or perfection or the satisfaction of the individual is achieved not by satisfying the ego but in a larger self. The ego is a smallness of being. It is a contraction of the consciousness which leads to limitation of knowledge, disabling ignorance, loss of oneness, disharmony, failure of sympathy love and understanding, fragmentation of delight of being and pain and sorrow. The larger self is infinite, possessing unlimited knowledge and undivided oneness, harmony and unfragmented delight of being. To recover the true self one must break out of the ego. It must disappear in impersonality or fuse into the cosmic 'I' or the transcendent self.

The '*Jiva*' is a spirit superior to Nature. It consents to her acts and allows itself to be dominated by the changing conditions of mind, life and body. It is a soul – form of the spirit universal and transcendent. This spirit is the very self of our self. The aim of human life is to realize that, '*Jiva*' is not only a spiritual centre of our personality but a substance of the very substance of the supreme self. Up to this point, the traditional teachers agree with each other. They say that the supreme object of knowledge, works and devotion is that the '*Jiva*' must release itself from the ego-sense which belongs to the lower Nature or *Maya*. But on the question of the nature of this realization they differ from each other. The Advaitin fixes on the path of an exclusive knowledge. His goal is an entire return and an extinction of the '*Jiva*' in the supreme. Both the Dvaitin and the Visistadvaitin turn to the path of devotion and say that, by shedding the lower ego, the '*Jiva*' realizes its nature as an eternal existence absorbed in thought, love and enjoyment of God.

For the seeker of the Integral Yoga, the ego is a limiting factor which has to be dissolved. The dissolution of the ego enables the true self to come to the surface. He seeks the integral knowledge and reaches the utmost height. He also spreads to the largest wideness and contains the soul's highest and greatest spiritual experiences. He insists upon the absolute union of the soul with the highest which exceeds the individual and the universe. This is also must be the goal even if he chooses the path of action or devotion. The path of action is not fulfilled if he has not realized the integral oneness of the Divine. As the instrument of the Divine he works for the sake of the Divine. The culmination of works is reached when he realizes oneness with that which he serves. The path of devotion is also complete when the Lover and the Beloved are unified and difference is abolished in the divine oneness. As Sri Aurobindo says, "we come to the realization of the spirit, the self, lord of this individual human manifestation, self but our knowledge is not integral if we do not make this self in the individual one with the cosmic spirit and find their greater reality above in an inexpressible but not unknowable, Transcendence."[6]

There will be no ego-sense for the integral seeker even if there is a sort of individualization in an individual mind and frame. All will be the one and every person will be the one in many forms. He works as divine instrument in order to fulfill the will of God in the world without any trace of the ego-sense. He has exceeded the ego which is not indispensable to the world play. To quote Sri Aurobindo:

> It is the integral knowledge and not anything either half-way and attractive or high-pinnacled and exclusive he (the disciple of the Integral Yoga) must seek. He must soar to the utmost height, but also circle and spread to the most all-embracing wideness, not binding himself to any rigid structure of metaphysical thought, but free to admit and contain all the soul's highest and greatest and fullest and most numerous experiences. If the highest height of spiritual experience, the sheer summit of all realization is the absolute union of the soul with the Transcendent who exceeds the individual and the universe, the widest scope of that union is the discovery of that very Transcendent as the source, support, continent, informing and constituent spirit and substance of both these manifesting powers of the divine Essence and the divine Nature. Whatever the path, this must be for him the goal.[7]

Knowledge and Oneness

In the traditional path of knowledge, one has to discover one's true self by withdrawing from identification with the mind, life and body. Having discovered the oneness of the self with the pure immutable Brahman the individual soul escapes from its own personality into the impersonal Self or *Akshara Brahman*. On the way to this supreme realization, other realizations are possible. The seeker may realize the Lord of the universe, may arrive at the cosmic consciousness, may know and feel his unity with all beings. But these are to be considered only as stages of his journey towards the ultimate goal. Therefore, none of them is to be regarded as the final end. The ultimate goal of the seeker of this Yoga is to pass beyond all these lesser realizations and arrive at a release into the ineffable Reality.

For the seeker of the Integral Yoga, the ultimate goal is more comprehensive and looks upon the escape into the immutable Brahman as a partial realization. According to the traditional view, Being is one only in itself and not in all its poises and aspects. It is supposed to be one only in the principle of unity and not in the principle of multiplicity. Therefore, it excludes all other forms of reality and their corresponding realizations are inadequate for the purpose of reaching the Absolute oneness. As Sri Aurobindo points out, the Integral Yoga makes no such division. He says:

> It (the integral knowledge) finds the same oneness in the Unmanifest and the Manifest, in the Impersonal and the Personal, in Nirguna and Saguna, in the infinite depths of the universal silence and the infinite largeness of the universal action. It finds the same absolute oneness in the Purusha and

> the Prakriti; in the divine Presence and the works of the divine Power and Knowledge; in the eternal manifestness of the one Purusha and the constant manifestation of the many Purushas; in the inalienable unity of Sachchidananda keeping constantly real to itself its own manifold oneness and in the apparent divisions of mind, life and body in which oneness is constantly, if secretly real and constantly seeks to be realized. All unity is to it an intense, pure and infinite realization, all difference and abundant, rich and boundless realization of the same divine and eternal Being.[8]

Therefore, the seeker lives in the consciousness of the transcendent Absolute and of the Absolute manifested in all relations. He finds the Supreme Being knowing all, governing all as the *purusha* and at the same time executing all knowledge, will and formation as *prakriti*. He also finds Him as one mind containing all mental beings, one Life active in all living beings and one Matter constituting all forms and objects. He realizes that the present human nature is only an imperfect expression of the divine nature which is gradually evolving in order to replace the former. To him the advent of a divine life on earth is inevitable and the integral oneness is the foundation upon which the advent of a new life upon earth is based.

The Integral Yoga represents the unity of the aims set before themselves by the three paths of knowledge, works and devotion. Knowledge aims at the realization of true self existence, *sat*, works aims at the realization of the divine will behind all works, *chit-tapas*. Devotion aims at realization of Bliss which supports all being and existences, *ananda*. The goal of the Integral Yoga is a triune realization of Sachchidananda through a natural unification of knowledge, works and devotion.

Knowledge helps the integral seeker to arrive at the possibility of the divine action through the consciousness of the Lord of the world. In this sense, it becomes the fulfillment of the path of works. In the same way knowledge reveals to us the glory and beauty of the Beloved everywhere to whom all beings are attracted by a passion of universal delight and a joy of universal love. In this sense it represents the summit of the path of Devotion. The integral knowledge is not merely the knowledge of the Divine beyond the world but of the Divine which lives and upholds the various forms of the world. The Divine is one not only in the transcendent state but also in the dynamic manifestation of the world. In this sense, it is the culmination of the traditional path of knowledge.

Knowledge and Liberation

To become free from death and therefore, free from birth also and to achieve immortality is possible in other worlds or on higher planes of existence. Naturally, if one is to be liberated into immortality one must do so by destroying all possibility of mental or bodily living or the individual existence in an impersonal infinity. There is a certain truth in this view because when the soul gives up the ties of mind and matter it feels an upward attraction resulting in a dense of a real self-existence to be possessed elsewhere and not here. As long as one is part of earthly living one has to submit to the ties of matter and mind and to a constant dying imposed by them. If immortality is a reality, it must be available in some immaterial plane and not here, in some higher plane where the body does not exist or is different if a body exists.

The ideal of the path of '*Jnana*' can be stated in another form also. Life upon earth is impossible without the ego. By its very nature the ego is a principle of dependence. It depends on the idea of God, personal self and other beings. But in reality, the soul exists absolutely and independently in itself. It does not depend upon God, personal self and other beings. Therefore, to realize the absolute independence it has to reject its dependence on God or other beings. In the same way, it has to reject its dependence on personal self because the persistence of ego is an admission of that which it tries to exclude as not-self. Whether absolute independence of the self or an immortal life which is beyond the cycle of births and deaths, the seeker of the path of knowledge has to dissolve the bodily existence and the reality of personal self by dissolving the ego.

From the point of view of integral knowledge, when we break out from ego and physical mind into the infinity of the spirits, we still see the world and others as before. The world and others seem to be quite opposite impersonality of spiritual existence and nothing else matters. So, there is a tendency to look upon the world and others as unreal and worthless entities. However, a release from ego need not necessarily encourage a withdrawal from the world and the other human beings. The other alternative is that, he who is free from ego is better equipped to acquire a proper relationship with the world and others. This is what the seeker of the Integral Yoga tries to achieve. In him the realized soul returns upon the world and a free possession of the outer nature by the inner spirit becomes possible. The world and others become to him realities of the eternal. To quote Sri Aurobindo on the change of attitude of the integral seeker in respect of the world outside.

> Our minds are no longer subject to the delusion of trivial unworthiness or the illusion of unreality.

> The material life loses indeed for us its old absorbing value, but finds the greater value which it has for the divine Purusha; regarded no longer as the sole term of our becoming, but as merely having a subordinate value in relation to the higher terms of mind and spirit, it increases by that diminution instead of losing in value. We see that our material being, life, nature are only one poise of the Purusha in relation to its Prakriti and that their true purpose and importance can only be appreciated when they are seen not as a thing in itself, but as dependent on higher poises by which they are supported; from those superior relations they derive their meaning and, therefore, by conscious union with them they can fulfill all their valid tendencies and aims. Life then becomes justified to us and no longer stultified by the possession of liberated self-knowledge.[9]

The integral knowledge aimed at by the integral seeker, harmonizes the three terms of God, ourselves and the world. They are no longer inconsistent or incompatible. They are also not terms of ignorance. In fact, they are terms of fulfillment in which their value is preserved.

When the ego disappears into an infinite being in which we no longer feel bound to the name and form, our present birth and becoming. This is what the ancients called the non-birth. One continues to live and act through his individual birth and becoming but with a difference. The world is seen in one's own being and not as something external to oneself. To live in this consciousness is to attain liberation and enjoy immortality.

Knowledge and Samadhi

Samadhi or yogic trance is considered by the seeker

of the yoga of knowledge as a kind of immersion in immobile, timeless and infinite being. It is in trance that, the soul departs into the silence of the highest state of being. On reaching the highest state in trance the soul does not see any possibility of return into any inferior state of existence.

In the old Indian tradition, consciousness is referred to as having four levels: *jagrat*, *svapna*, *susupti* and *turiya*. *Jagrat* is the waking state, the consciousness of the material universe which we normally possess through the physical mind. *Svapna* is the dream state, the consciousness corresponding to the subtler life-plane and mind-plane behind the physical world. *Susupti* is the sleep-state, the consciousness corresponding to the supramental plane. Because our causal body is not fully developed in us we cannot enter into any relationship with that plane during the sleep-state. *Turiya* is a far higher level than the previous one. It is a state of an absolute being with which we have no direct relations at all either in the waking state or in the dream state or in the sleep-state. To get back from the physical mind to the absolute being one has to withdraw from the waking state. Otherwise, it is not possible to rise to that level. Since the traditional path of knowledge proceeds from the physical mind to the highest reality of being, trance becomes necessary as a means of escape from the limitations of the physical mind.

For the seeker of the Integral Yoga, the method of *samadhi* has a disadvantage. The soul is in relation with the highest states of being only when he is drawn into the yogic trance. When he comes out of that trance, he cannot remember anything that he possessed in trance. The outer life remains totally untouched by the trance experiences. Therefore, when he comes out of the trance state he behaves as if he is one of the ignorant men in the society.

He is forced to lead a double life, a life inside and a totally different life outside. But for the seeker of the Integral Yoga, the gulf between the inner and the outer life does not exist. By contrast, the integral seeker has two advantages. In the words of Sri Aurobindo:

> In the first place, it is only in the untrained psychic being that the experiences of the trance are a blank to the waking mind; as it becomes the master of its Samadhi, it is able to pass without any gulf of oblivion from the inner to the outer waking. Secondly, when this has been once done, what is attained in the inner state, becomes easier to acquire by the waking consciousness and to turn into the normal experience, powers, mental status of the waking life.[10]

What is gained in *samadhi* is not restricted to an existence beyond the waking life, but extended to the waking consciousness which makes it as a normal possession and experience.

REFERENCES

1. *S.Y.*, p. 267.
2. *Ibid.*, p. 265.
3. *Ibid.*, p. 295.
4. *Ibid.*, p. 295.
5. *Ibid.*, pp. 306-307.
6. *Ibid.*, p. 335.
7. *Ibid.*, p. 334.
8. *Ibid.*, p. 389.
9. *Ibid.*, p. 410.
10. *Ibid.*, p. 487.

CHAPTER 12

INTEGRAL YOGA AND THE YOGA OF DEVOTION

Devotion and the Triple Path

Generally, the way of devotion is considered to be inferior because it implies worship and worship belongs to a condition where there is a difference between the human soul and the Divine. Love and dualism are inseparable because without the dualism of the lover and the beloved love becomes impossible. Therefore, it is said that the path of devotion is only for souls that are not yet ready for the highest truth.

Like the *Jnani*, the *bhakta* looks down upon knowledge as a mere mental perception. Knowledge is clear but dry without rapture of spiritual experience. Therefore, the devotee considers that knowledge is inferior to devotion. If knowledge aims at an abstract light through a liberated consciousness, devotion insists on a deep ecstasy of union. For a devotee the ecstatic union has no parallel. Therefore, he is not enamoured of knowledge which cannot offer the ecstasy born of passionate union.

Both knowledge and devotion look down on the way of works as inferior to their own loftier spiritual achievement. Because works are considered to be something outward and therefore, distracts the soul from its exclusive oneness with the Divine.

From the point of view of the integral seeker, the path of devotion cannot be considered inferior to other paths. When the devotee has laid hold on love, it purifies and enlarges him as effectively as knowledge can. It is true that devotion and knowledge differ in their methods, but in their aim they do not. As Sri Aurobindo rightly points out:

> When the devotee has grasped the power that shall raise him, has really laid hold on love, that in the end purifies and enlarges him as effectively as knowledge can; they are equal powers, though their methods of arriving at the same goal are different. The pride of the philosopher looking down on the passion of the devotee arises, as does all pride, from a certain deficiency of his nature; for the intellect too exclusively developed misses what the heart has to offer. The intellect is not in every way superior to the heart; if it opens more readily doors at which the heart is apt to fumble in vain, it is, itself, apt to miss truths which to the heart are very near and easy to hold. And if when the way of thought deepens into spiritual experience, it arrives readily at the etherial heights, pinnacles, skyey widenesses, it cannot without the aid of the heart fathom the intense and rich abysses and oceanic depths of the divine being and the divine Ananda.[1]

The Integral Yoga points out that, it is true that knowledge cannot give all the satisfaction we seek as long as it has not left its supports of thought and crosses beyond the mind. But it is also true that devotion itself is not complete without knowledge. The Gita distinguishes between three kinds of devotion, *arta, artharthi* and *jijnasu*. To seek refuge in the Divine from the sorrows of the world is *arta*. To approach the Divine as the giver of the good is *artharthi*. To be attracted by what the soul loves but does not yet know is *jijnasu*. Therefore, the Gita tells us that devotion becomes complete when it reaches the oneness of consciousness which is knowledge, *Jijnasu*. Devotion and knowledge are not exclusive of each other. As knowledge of the divine grows delight in the Divine increases. Devotion leading to rapture is not secure without the foundation of knowledge. Sri Aurobindo says:

> Nor can mere rapture be secure without the foundation of knowledge; to live in what we love, gives that security, and to live in it means to be one with it in consciousness and oneness of consciousness in the perfect condition of knowledge. Knowledge of the Divine gives to love of the Divine its firmest security, opens to it its own widest joy of experience, raises it to its highest pinnacles of outlook.[2]

If knowledge is the state of oneness and devotion, the bliss resulting from that oneness, divine works are the living power of the light and sweetness involved in that oneness and bliss. As Sri Aurobindo says, works are the "very power of knowledge and the very outpouring of love".[3] For the integral seeker, works cannot be outward or distracting because he has found his oneness of will and consciousness with the Divine.

Devotion and Divine Love

There are four stages in the Yoga of devotion: (1) The desire of the soul towards God, (2) The pain of love and the divine return of Love, (3) The delight of love possessed and the play of that delight, and (4) The eternal enjoyment of the divine lover. These are four successive stages of the Yoga of devotion. The aim of this Yoga is union with the Divine through some kind of touch or closeness or possession. Initially, the desire for union is formulated through outward worship. But when this adoration leads to a change of consciousness, it becomes an inner worship. The devotee considers himself as a temple of the Divine. His thoughts and feelings become a prayer of aspiration and seeking. His entire life becomes an external service. The Yoga of devotion results in a sort of liberation by likeness to the Divine *Sadrsya-mukti*. It uses human relations — the relations of the master and the servant, the father and the child, the mother and the child and the lover and the beloved — to realize union with the Divine. These relations are capable of raising man to the highest spiritual level because human relations are only imperfect but still the real type of divine relations of God and the human soul.

From the point of view of the Integral Yoga, the Yoga of devotion must take into itself the essential elements of the Yoga of works and knowledge. When the Yoga of devotion is a sacrifice of life and works to the Divine rather than a furning of the will to the Divine will, the devotee offers his life, his capacities and possessions to the Divine. He accepts the fullness of life and the world in its entity as the play of the Divine and does all works as an offering to Him. There is not merely a consecration of one's activities but also the thoughts to the Divine. Strictly speaking, this is the devotion of the mind. There are three stages to it: (1) Constant hearing of the Divine name, qualifies and all that has been attached to them; (2) Constant thinking on the Divine name or qualities; and (3) Fixing of the mind on the Divine. It seeks not to pass into the being of the Divine. On the contrary, it brings the Divine into the devotee and the devotee loses himself in the ecstasy of his presence.

The traditional yoga of devotion, from the point of view of the integral seeker, includes not only the yoga of works and knowledge but a positive emphasis on the fullness of life and the world. There is no longer the ascetic tendency to turn away from life and the world. The integral seeker realizes that the divine is not only within but also everywhere. To quote Sri Aurobindo:

> He is sought within in the heart and therefore apart from all by an inward-gathered concentration of the being in the soul itself; but he is also seen and loved everywhere where he manifests his being. All the beauty and joy of existence is seen as his joy and beauty; he is embraced by the spirit in all beings; the ecstasy of love enjoyed pours itself out in a universal love; all existence becomes a radiation of its delight and even in its very appearances is transformed into something other than its outward appearance.[4]

In the way of knowledge there is a tendency towards the impersonal Reality. And so, it is likely to become exclusive. Though an integral realization of unity is possible, it is not quite imperative. In the same way, the way of works leads to an identification with the Transcendent Divine whose power manifest itself as a will in the world. Naturally, there is certain comprehensiveness in this realization. But this is not quite imperative, because the motive of union may be detached in its principle although there is a continued participation in the activities of the universal Godhead. When the principle of delight becomes pronounced the motive of integral union becomes quite imperative. The way of love leads to an integral delight which embraces the Divine in all its aspects of transcendence universality and individuality. To quote Sri Aurobindo:

> By knowledge we seek unity with the Divine in his conscious being: by works we seek also unity with the Divine in his conscious being, not statically, but dynamically, through conscious union with the divine Will; but by love we seek unity with him in all the delight of his being. For that reason the way of love, however narrow it may seem in some of its first movements, is in the end more imperatively all-embracing than any other motive of Yoga.[5]

REFERENCES

1. *S.Y.*, p. 510.
2. *Ibid.*, p. 512.
3. *Ibid.*, p. 512.
4. *Ibid.*, p. 537.
5. *Ibid.*, p. 549.

Chapter 13

Integral Yoga and the Other Yogas

Hathayoga

Like all other Yogas, hathayoga emphasises three important things:

*(1) **Purification:*** It is removal of all disorders and the irregular action of energy in our physical, moral and mental system.

*(2) **Concentration:*** It is the employment of energy of being in us for a specific goal.

*(3) **Liberation:*** It is release of our being from its narrowness and false limitations. Liberation leads to an union with the supreme.

There are two aspects to the physical discipline of hathayoga. They are *asana* and *pranayama*. *Asana* is a process of training the body in order to acquire certain attitude of immobility. *Pranayama* is a regulated direction and arrestation by exercise of breathing. These two, *asana* and *pranayama* are respectively concerned with the two aspects of the physical being. The body and the vital energy are the two aspects. The body is the apparent instrument and basis, while the vital energy is the power and the real instrument. The aim of this Yoga is to achieve mastery in respect of the above two parts of the physical being.

There is enormous variety of *asanas* in hathayoga. The gross body is trained with the help of these *asanas*. As a result, the gross body acquires something of the nature of the subtle body and of its relations with life energy. *Pranayama* is concerned with the nervous system and is done by various regulations of breathing process. A combination of *asanas* and *pranayama* leads to a high level of perfection of the health of the body. Hathayoga gives to the soul in the physical body the power, the light, the purity and the freedom which would naturally open to it if it dwelt in the subtle part of the body. This is the basic aim of this Yoga. As Sri Aurobindo says of the attitude of the hathayoga towards human body:

> The body is the key, the body the secret both of bondage and of release, of animal weakness and of divine power, of the obscuration of the mind and soul and of their illumination, of subjection to pain and limitation and of self-mastery, of death and of immortality.[1]

Rajayoga

Whereas, hathayoga starts with the body, rajayoga starts with the mind. It begins with a moral purification of mentality. It is very important because without it in the following stages of discipline are likely to be marred by mental, moral and physical dangers. According to rajayoga, the moral purification is effected through two steps: moral discipline (*yama*) and religious observances (*niyama*). In fact, *yama* is a self-discipline by which the *rajasic* egoism and its desires are brought under complete control. *Yama* includes non-injury (*ahimsa*), truth-speaking (*satya*), abstention from stealing (*asteya*), celibacy (*brahmacarya*) and disowning of possessions (*aparigraha*). In the same way, *niyama* is also the discipline of the mind in order to create a *sattwik* calm and purity for concentration on higher forms of meditation. It includes purity (*shauca*), contentment (*santosha*), fortitude (*tapas*), study (*svadhyaya*) and devotion to God (*ishwara-pramidhana*). Though, *yama* and *niyama* purify the system, they cannot bring out the psychic being which is necessary for progress in Yoga. This is achieved by *pranayama*, though *asana* plays a secondary role in the process. Then come the four stages of concentration: (1) Drawing of the mind and senses from outward things (*pratyahara*); (2) Holding of one object of concentration to the exclusion of other ideas and mental activities (*dharana*); (3) Prolonged absorption of the mind in the object of concentration (*dhyana*); and (4) Complete ingoing of the object leading to oneness (*samadhi*). The aim of this Yoga is to still the waves of consciousness and its activities, *Chittavrttinirodhah*. When thought ceases the mind frees itself from the outward and the mental world into union with the Divine Being.

From the stand point of the Integral Yoga the results of rajayoga and hathayoga are very important though they can be achieved by other means. Sri Aurobindo says:

> It is true that their principal aims must be included in the integrality of the Yoga; but they can be brought about by other means. For the methods

> of the integral Yoga must be mainly spiritual, and dependence on physical methods or fixed psychic or psycho-physical processes on a large scale would be the substitution of a lower for a higher action.[2]

The Integral Yoga of Sri Aurobindo insists that, the largest development of spiritual power and transformation of the whole human nature by it can be achieved by the shortest way without going through the complex processes of hathayoga or depending excessively on abnormal states of trance of rajayoga.

Tantrayoga

Tantrayoga may be distinguished from other Yogas which have origin in the vedantic tradition. The Yogas which are vedantic in principle consider that their force is knowledge and their method is also knowledge. In them the chief instrument is the *purusha,* the soul that knows, observes and governs. But in *tantrayoga,* it is *prakriti* which is important. It achieves its fourfold aim of mastery, perfection, liberation and beatitude by discovering and using the secret of *prakriti* or will in power.

The main aim of tantric yoga is to raise nature in man into manifest power of spirit. It uses the methods of hathayoga and rajayoga for achieving this aim, though not limited by their methods. It uses the hathayogic process of *pranayama* to open up the nervous centers and the rajayogic methods of purification, meditation and concentration to liberate the mind from its limitations. There are two things which distinguish the tantric discipline. To quote Sri Aurobindo:

> First, it lays its hand firmly on many of the main springs of human quality, desire, action and it subjects them to an intensive discipline with the

> soul's mastery of its motives as a first aim and their elevation to a diviner spiritual level as its final utility. Again, it includes in its objects of Yoga not only liberation, which is the one all-mastering preoccupation of the specific systems, but a cosmic enjoyment of the power of the Spirit, which the others may take incidentally on the way, in part, casually, but avoid making a motive or object.[3]

From the point of view of the Integral Yoga, the results of the tantric yoga can be realized through the methods of other Yogas which are vedantic in origin and principle because in tantric yoga one is prone to be lost in its principle and machinery and the discipline become a thing of formulae and occult mechanism. The tantric methods relies on *shakti* as the all-important. *Shakti* is the key to the finding of spirit. But the Integral Yoga proceeds on the understanding of man as a spirit in mind rather than a spirit in body. It depends on the power of the soul in mind as the key to the spiritual progress. In other words, the Integral Yoga starts with the power of the spirit in mind and achieves all the results of the tantric yoga which realizes its goal through the power of the spirit in the body, '*Kundalini Shakti*'. In the words of Sri Aurobindo, the Integral Yoga "starts from the method of Vedanta to arrive at the aim of the Tantra".[4]

REFERENCES

1. *S.Y.*, p. 491.
2. *Ibid.*, p. 504.
3. *Ibid.*, pp. 571-572.
4. *Ibid.*, p. 572.

Bibliography

I. Works by Sri Aurobindo

Sri Aurobindo, *Lights on Yoga*, Sri Aurobindo Library, Howrah, 1935.

Sri Aurobindo, *Bases of Yoga*, Arya Publishing House, Calcutta, 1936.

Sri Aurobindo, *Hymns to the Mystic Fire*, Sri Aurobindo Ashram, Pondicherry, 1946.

Sri Aurobindo, *More Lights on Yoga*, Sri Aurobindo Ashram, Pondicherry, 1948.

Sri Aurobindo, *The Human Cycle*, Sri Aurobindo Ashram, Pondicherry, 1949.

Sri Aurobindo, *The Life Divine*, Sri Aurobindo Library, INC., New York, 1949.

Sri Aurobindo, *The Ideal of Human Unity*, Sri Aurobindo Ashram, Pondicherry, 1950.

Sri Aurobindo, *The Riddle of this World*, Sri Aurobindo Ashram, Pondicherry, 1951.

Sri Aurobindo, *The Supramental Manifestation upon Earth*, Sri Aurobindo Ashram, Pondicherry, 1952.

Sri Aurobindo, *The Problem of Rebirth*, Sri Aurobindo Ashram, Pondicherry, 1952.

Sri Aurobindo, *Sri Aurobindo on Himself and on the Mother*, Sri Aurobindo Ashram, Pondicherry, 1953.

Sri Aurobindo, *Thoughts and Aphorisms*, Sri Aurobindo Ashram, Pondicherry, 1959.

Sri Aurobindo, *The Hour of God*, Sri Aurobindo Ashram, Pondicherry, 1964.

Sri Aurobindo, *On the Veda*, Sri Aurobindo Ashram, Pondicherry, 1964.

Sri Aurobindo, *The Synthesis of Yoga*, Sri Aurobindo Ashram, Pondicherry, 1965.

Sri Aurobindo, *The Foundation of Indian Culture*, Sri Aurobindo Ashram, Pondicherry, 1968.

Sri Aurobindo, *Letters on Yoga*, Sri Aurobindo Ashram, Pondicherry, 1969.

Sri Aurobindo, *Essays on the Gita*, Sri Aurobindo Ashram, Pondicherry, 1970.

Sri Aurobindo, *The Secret of the Veda*, Sri Aurobindo Ashram, Pondicherry, 1971.

II. Works by Others

Bahadur, K.P., *The Wisdom of Yoga*, Sterling Publishers Private Limited, New Delhi, 1977.

Bharati, Agehananada, *The Tantric Tradition*, B.I. Publications, Madras, 1976.

Chandrasekharam, Velury, *Sri Aurobindo's Life Divine: A Brief Study*, Sri Aurobindo Ashram, Pondicherry, 1973.

Chatterjee, S., and Datta, D.M., *An Introduction to Indian Philosophy*, University of Calcutta, Calcutta, 1968.

Chincholkar, L.G., *A Critical Study of Aurobindo*, Anante Bhawan, Dhantoli, Nagpur, 1966.

Damodaran, K., *Indian Thought: A Critical Survey*, Asia Publishing House, Bombay, 1967.

Dasgupta, S.N., *Yoga Philosophy*, Motilal Banarasidass, Delhi, 1974.

Datta, D.M., *The Chief Currents of Contemporary Philosophy*, University of Calcutta, Calcutta, 1961.

Dilipkumar Roy, *Sri Aurobindo Came to Me*, Sri Aurobindo Ashram, Pondicherry, 1952.

Diwakar, R.R., *Mahayogi*, Bharatiya Vidya Bhavan, Bombay, 1954.

Gupta, Nolini Kanta, *The Yoga of Sri Aurobindo*, Sri Aurobindo Ashram, Pondicherry, 1983.

Gupta, Nolini Kanta, *The Approach to Mysticism*, Sri Aurobindo Ashram, Pondicherry, 1946.

Haridas Chaudhuri, *Sri Aurobindo: The Prophet of Life Divine*, Sri Aurobindo Ashram, Pondicherry, 1973.

Haridas Chaudhuri, *Integral Yoga*, George Allen and Unwin, London, 1965.

Haridas Chaudhuri, *The Philosophy of Integralism*, Sri Aurobindo Ashram, Pondicherry, 1967.

Hiriyanna, M., *Outlines of Indian Philosophy*, George Allen and Unwin, India, 1973.

Hume, Robert Ernest, *The Thirteen Principal Upanishads*, Oxford University Press, London, 1958.

Iyengar, K.R. Srinivasa, *Sri Aurobindo: A Biography and a*

History, vol. I and II, Sri Aurobindo International Centre of Education, Pondicherry, 1972.

James Haughton Woods, *Yoga System of Patanjali*, Motilal Banarasidass, Delhi, 1972.

Joseph Leeming, *Yoga and the Bible*, George Allen and Unwin, London, 1963.

Kapali Sastry, T.V., *Lights on the Upanishads*, Pondicherry, 1959.

Karan Singh, *Prophet of Indian Nationalism*, George Allen and Unwin, London, 1963.

Keshavmurti, *Sri Aurobindo – The Hope of Man*, Sri Aurobindo Ashram, Pondicherry, 1969.

Kewal Motwani, *Three Great Sages*, Ganesh and Co., Madras, 1951.

Madhusudan Reddy, V., *Sri Aurobindo's Philosophy of Evolution*, Institute of Human Study, Hyderabad, 1966.

Mahadevan, T.M.P., and Saroja, G.V., *Contemporary Indian Philosophy*, Sterling Publishers Private Limited, Delhi, 1981.

Mahadevan, T.M.P., *The Philosophy of Advaita*, Luzac and Co., London, 1938.

Mahadevan, T.M.P., *Outlines of Hinduism*, Chetana Ltd., Bombay, 1960.

Maitra, S.K., *The Meeting of the East and the West in Sri Aurobindo's Philosophy*, Sri Aurobindo Ashram, Pondicherry, 1956.

Maitra, S.K., *An Introduction to the Philosophy of Sri Aurobindo*, Sri Aurobindo Ashram, Pondicherry, 1982.

Misra, Ram Shankar, *The Integral Advaitism of Sri Aurobindo*, Banaras Hindu University, Banaras, 1957.

Morwenna Donnelly, *Founding the Life Divine* (An Introduction to the Integral Yoga of Sri Aurobindo), Hawthorn Books, INC., New York, 1956.

Mouni Sadhu, *Samadhi*, George Allen and Unwin, London, 1962.

Mukherjee, J.K., *The Destiny of the Body*, Sri Aurobindo Ashram, Pondicherry, 1975.

Naravane, V.S., *Modern Indian Thought*, Asia Publishing House, Bombay, 1964.

Narayan Prasad, *Life in Sri Aurobindo Ashram*, Sri Aurobindo Ashram, Pondicherry, 1968.

Nathaniel Pearson, *Sri Aurobindo and the Soul Quest of Man*, George Allen and Unwin, London, 1952.

Nirodbaran, *Correspondence with Sri Aurobindo*, Sri Aurobindo Ashram, Pondicherry, 1969.

Pandit, M.P., *Highways of God*, Sri Aurobindo, Study Circle, Madras, 1950.

Pandit, M.P., *Kundalini Yoga*, Ganesh and Co., Madras, 1959.

Pandit, M.P., *Sri Aurobindo: A Survey*, Sri Aurobindo Ashram, Pondicherry, 1972.

Pandit, M.P., *Sadhana in Sri Aurobindo's Yoga*, Sri Aurobindo Ashram, Pondicherry, 1978.

Pandia, M.P., *Lights on the Tantra*, Ganesh and Co., Madras, 1957.

Purani, A.B., *Sri Aurobindo: Addresses on His Life and Teachings*, Sri Aurobindo Ashram, Pondicherry, 1955.

Purani, A.B., *The Life of Sri Aurobindo*, Sri Aurobindo Ashram, Pondicherry, 1964.

Purani, A.B., *Sri Aurobindo's Life Divine*, Sri Aurobindo Ashram, Pondicherry, 1966.

Purani, A.B., *Technical Terms of Sri Aurobindo's Philosophy*, Sri Aurobindo Ashram, Pondicherry, 1949.

Radhakrishnan, S., *The Bhagavad Gita*, George Allen and Unwin, London, 1958.

Radhakrishnan, S., *Indian Philosophy*, vol. I and II, George Allen and Unwin, London, 1966.

Ram Nath Sharma, *The Philosophy of Sri Aurobindo*, Kedar Nath Ram Nath, Meerut, 1963.

Rishabhchand, *The Integral Yoga of Sri Aurobindo*, Sri Aurobindo Ashram, Pondicherry, 1959.

Saint-Hilarire, P.B., *The Future Evolution of Man*, George Allen and Unwin, London, 1963.

Satprem, *Sri Aurobindo or the Adventure of Consciousness*, Sri Aurobindo Ashram, Pondicherry, 1973.

Sethana, K.D., *The Vision and Work of Sri Aurobindo*, Sri Aurobindo Ashram, Pondicherry, 1968.

Sharma, D.S., *Studies in the Renaissance of Hinduism*, Banaras Hindu University, Banaras, 1944.

Sharma, Chandradhar, *A Critical Survey of Indian Philosophy*, Motilal Banarasidass, Delhi, 1976.

Sri John Woodroffe, *Shakti and Shakta*, Ganesh and Co., Madras, 1959.

Sri John Woodroffe, *Principles of Tantra*, Part I and II, Ganesh and Co., Madras, 1978.

Sri John Woodroffe, *Introduction to Tantra Sastra*, Ganesh and Co., Madras, 1980.

Srinivasachari, P.N., *The Wisdom of the Upanishads*, Sri Krishna Library, Madras, 1947.

Srinivasachari, P.N., *The Philosophy of Visistadvaita*, The Adyar Library and Research Centre, Madras, 1970.

Srivastava, R.S., *Contemporary Indian Philosophy*, Munshiram Manoharlal, Delhi, 1965.

Swami Gambhirananda, *Eight Upanishads*, vol. I and II, Advaita Ashram, Calcutta, 1972, 1973.

Swami Nikhilananda (tr.), *The Gospel of Sri Ramakrishna*, Sri Ramakrishna Math, Madras, 1972.

Swami Prabhavananda, *The Spiritual Heritage of India*, George Allen and Unwin, London, 1962.

Swami Vivekananda, *The Complete works of Swami Vivekananda*, vol. I to VIII, Mayavati Memorial Edition.

The Mother, *Conversions*, Sri Aurobindo Ashram, Pondicherry, 1973.

Tilak, B.G., *Gita Rahasya*, Tilak Brothers, Poona, 1977.

Tulsidas Chatterjee, *Sri Aurobindo's Integral Yoga*, New Rooplekha Press, Calcutta, 1970.

Varma, V.P., *The Political Philosophy of Sri Aurobindo*, Asia Publishing House, Bombay, 1960.

Woods, James Haughton, *The Yoga System of Patanjali*, Motilal Banarasidass, Delhi, 1972.

Zaehner, R.C., *The Bhagavad Gita*, Oxford University Press, 1969.

III. Articles in Journals

Anilbaran Roy, "Concept of God in Patanjali", Sri Aurobindo Circle, 1946.

Arabinda Basu, "Liberation and Transformation", Sri Aurobindo Circle, 1961.

Chubb, J.N., "Sri Aurobindo – His Life and Teachings", Sri Aurobindo Circle, 1962.

Crampton Chalk, A.L., "Sacrifice and Egoism", Sri Aurobindo Circle, 1950.

Crampton Chalk, A.L., "Annihilation of Ego", Sri Aurobindo Circle, 1954.

Haridas Chaudhuri, "The Aim of Integral Yoga", Sri Aurobindo Mandir Annual, 1946.

Haridas Chaudhuri, "The Main Principles of Integral Yoga", Sri Aurobindo Circle, 1947.

India, C.T., "Sri Aurobindo's Renaissance in India", Triveni, October-December, 1983.

Indrasen, "Sri Aurobindo as a World Philosopher", Advent, August, 1984.

Jayashanmukam, N., "Evolution: Vertical and Horizontal", Indian Philosophical Annual, vol. 8, 1972.

Jugal Kishore Banerji, "Mathematics and Yoga", Sri Aurobindo Circle, 1956.

Jugal Kishore Mukherji, "The Yoga of Sri Aurobindo: Seven Limbs of a Sincere Call", Sri Aurobindo Circle, 1961.

Kapali Sastry, T.V., "Sidelights on Tantra", Sri Aurobindo Circle, 1950.

Pandit, M.P., "Sri Aurobindo's Concept of Evolution", Advent, August, 1984.

Pandit, M.P., "The Life Divine", Advent, August, 1984.

Pandit, M.P., "Sri Aurobindo as the Culmination of India's Spiritual Tradition", Advent, November, 1983.

Pandit, M.P., "Our Yoga and the Challenge of Pragmatism", Sri Aurobindo Circle, 1949.

Pandit, M.P., "Sri Aurobindo and the Upanishads", Sri Aurobindo Circle, 1984, 1955.

Pandit, M.P., "Our Yoga and the Tantra", Sri Aurobindo Circle, 1960.

Pandit, M.P., "Principles of Tantra", Sri Aurobindo Circle, 1961.

Pandit, M.P., "The Psychic Being", Sri Aurobindo Circle, 1962.

Pavitra, "To a Beginner in Yoga", Sri Aurobindo Circle, 1947.

Purani, A.B., "Sri Aurobindo and His Yoga Sadhana", Sri Aurobindo Circle, 1952.

Richard Stein, "The Yoga of Transformation", Advent, August, 1984.

Rishabhchand, "Life and its Ascent", Sri Aurobindo Circle, 1961.

Rishabhchand, "The Double Lever of Ascent", Sri Aurobindo Circle, 1962.

Rutledge Tompkins, "What the Integral Yoga Means to Me", Sri Aurobindo Circle, 1962.

Siddhinathananda, "The Descent of the Divine", The Vedanta Kesari, August, 1984.

Surya, "What Sri Aurobindo Means to Me", Advent, April, 1984.

Susmita Prasad Pain, "Sri Aurobindo's New Approach to the Study of the Veda", Advent, April, 1984.

Swami Saradananda, "An Introduction to the Study of the Gita", The Vedanta Kesari, January-February, 1985.

Varadachari, K.C., "Divine Evolutionism", Sri Aurobindo Mandir, Annual, 1942.

Varadachari, K.C., "A Critique of the Pramares", Sri Aurobindo Mandir, Annual, 1948.

Index